Philippians

A Visual and Textual Guide

Also available in the High Definition Commentary series:

Romans: A Visual and Textual Guide

Also available from Steven E. Runge:

Lexham Discourse Hebrew Bible

Lexham High Definition Old Testament

Discourse Studies and Biblical Interpretation:
A Festschrift in Honor of Stephen H. Levinsohn

Introducing New Testament Discourse Grammar: Video Series

Discourse Grammar of the Greek New Testament:
A Practical Introduction for Teaching and Exegesis

Lexham Discourse Greek New Testament

Lexham High Definition New Testament

Visit Logos.com/Runge to learn more

Philippians

A Visual and Textual Guide

High Definition Commentary

Steven E. Runge

LEXHAM PRESS

Philippians: A Textual and Visual Guide
High Definition Commentary

Copyright 2014 Lexham Press

Lexham Press, 1313 Commercial St., Bellingham, WA 98225
LexhamPress.com

Print ISBN 978-1-57-799592-0

Visual Design: Shiloh Hubbard
Publisher/Editor: John D. Barry
Copy Editor: Francine VanWoudenberg Sikkema
Project Support: Jessi Strong
Cover Design: Josh Warren
Typesetting: ProjectLuz.com

Acknowledgments and Dedication

Several people played a key role in the development of this volume. Thanks first and foremost to Bob Pritchett, who had the idea to marry the insights from my work in discourse studies with the power of infographics. These incredible graphics were fashioned by Shiloh Hubbard, a very gifted member of the Logos team. John D. Barry's work in editing and overseeing the production of this volume is also to be commended. Finally, special thanks to Patrick C. Geracie for contributing a conceptual framework that helped shape my understanding of Philippians; I dedicate this volume to him.

Table of Contents

Introduction   1

Philippians 1   5

    Philippians 1:1–11   7

    Philippians 1:12–17   13

    Philippians 1:18–20   19

    Philippians 1:21–26   25

    Philippians 1:27–30   31

Philippians 2   37

    Philippians 2:1–4   39

    Philippians 2:5–11   45

    Philippians 2:12–18   51

    Philippians 2:19–24   57

    Philippians 2:25–30   63

Philippians 3   69

    Philippians 3:1–4a   71

    Philippians 3:4b–11   75

    Philippians 3:12–14   83

    Philippians 3:15–21   89

Philippians 4   95

    Philippians 4:1–7   97

    Philippians 4:8–9   105

    Philippians 4:10–20   109

    Philippians 4:21–23   117

Final Reflections   119

Subject and Author Index   120

Scripture Index   123

About the Author   125

Introduction

How Is the High Definition Commentary Different?

What you are about to read is derived from a rigorous discourse analysis of the Greek text of Philippians. Discourse analysis doesn't just look at *what* is said but *how* it's said. By looking at how Paul phrased things in Greek, we can see the progression of his thoughts. The phrasing of every sentence in the New Testament presupposes decisions about communication—the same kinds of decisions we make every day.

This commentary guides you through the linguistic devices Paul used and shows what we can learn from them. It's a guided tour of the Greek text—minus the unnecessary details. I highlight the important stuff for you.

Why I Wrote This Commentary

Commentaries either give you the big picture or all the detail. But what I really want is a commentary that gives you the details you need without losing sight of the big picture. That's what this commentary is about.

In the *Lexham Discourse Greek New Testament* and the *Lexham High Definition New Testament*, I annotated all the significant discourse devices that aid us in biblical interpretation. There is one drawback to these volumes: The onus is on *you* to synthesize the data into a cohesive analysis. In this volume, I synthesize the conclusions that can be drawn from my analysis of Philippians and make them easy to understand.

Discourse studies have a reputation for complexity. Linguists joke that it rivals nuclear fission or brain surgery. The secret is that, as a speaker of any language, you actually know a lot more about discourse devices than you might think. The problem is that we rarely think about these issues. We just do what fits best in the context; we use whatever devices best communicate our message.

The Power of Discourse Analysis

Choice implies meaning. If I choose to say something *this way* as opposed to *that way*, I must have a reason for doing so. I can tackle these issues because of my analysis of the Greek New Testament and descriptions of discourse devices in the *Discourse Grammar of the Greek New Testament*. I do not claim to know what Paul was thinking or what he had in mind as he wrote. Such notions would be beyond presumptuous. Instead, I operate on the assumption that our use of language is based on our communication objectives. If we use a particular device that usually accomplishes a certain effect, then we can assume that the biblical writers used language in the same way. Ultimately, context is the final arbiter.

Most commentaries provide the scholar's interpretive conclusions using statements like "Paul is doing [fill in the blank] here." They give you the conclusion, but without showing you how they got there. This commentary is different. It helps you understand what is going on under the hood, linguistically speaking.

The primary job of pastors and teachers is exposition: drawing out the meaning of the text so that we can faithfully apply it to our lives. Like when I teach, my goal in this commentary is not just to give you the answers but to teach you how I found them. Why? Because I want you to find answers on your own.

In this commentary, I help you understand the flow of Paul's argument—to see how the pieces fit together into the whole. I do this because I want you to be able to teach others, whether that is in a small group, a Bible study, a class, or in a sermon.

Why Graphics?

Graphics represent ideas well, especially complex ones. The graphics in this commentary explain the text and help you (and others) retain its meaning.

Explaining

While the graphics in this commentary help you better understand a passage, the real target is the person you are teaching. The images help you explain key ideas using something other than a translation or a verbal description. They do not replace these things, but serve as another tool in your arsenal.

Retaining

Good graphics pay dividends into the future. Visual aids help us correlate and recall information. How many of your long-forgotten memories have been triggered by an old photo? We may not completely understand how the mind works, but visual signposts play a role in retention and recall. Most passages in this commentary have several graphics tied to a key idea. Some break a complex idea down into steps; others present a difficult idea in a new, memorable way.

My Goal for This Commentary

I want you to understand why Paul wrote Philippians and how he wrote it. I hope doing so changes your life like it has mine.

The electronic edition of the *High Definition Commentary: Philippians* is available for Logos Bible Software and includes ready-to-use versions of all the graphics for use in Proclaim, PowerPoint, and Keynote. You'll find it online at **Logos.com/HDCommentary**.

Philippians 1

Philippians 1:1–11

Introductions play a huge role in communication. In some Asian countries there is a formal protocol for exchanging business cards in introductions. In diplomacy, ambassadors present credentials to the host country from the nation they represent. In academic circles, the *curriculum vitae* is a formal résumé highlighting the scholar's significant achievements and qualifications. Each of these approaches accomplishes the same task: giving us the most important information we need to know about the person *for the particular context.* The fact that a person is the "Mid-Atlantic ballroom dancing champion" might be interesting, but would not be relevant in a diplomatic or academic setting.

In the context of introductions, we reveal the most relevant information the other person needs to know, based on the context. What would you think if I was introduced at the beginning of an academic lecture as "Ruth and Abby's dad," with no reference to my academic credentials? You might ask how this qualifies me as an expert. But if it was in the context of a soccer team barbeque, then being their dad may be the most relevant credential. So too with having a doctorate in an academic setting, and so on.

Understanding this principle of choosing the most relevant credential gives us insight into the various ways that Paul introduces himself in his letters. For example, in Galatians, where Paul's authority as an apostle is under attack, he introduces himself as "an apostle not from men nor by men but through Jesus Christ and God the Father who

Which One? When introductions are made in most cultures, some aspect about the person being introduced is provided. The one selected of all the options will be the one most relevant to the specific context. The same holds true for the letters in the New Testament. There are a number of different titles that Paul could have used to introduce himself to the audience. The credentials he cites vary from letter to letter, depending upon the themes and topics discussed. Choosing "slave of Christ" for Philippians fits well with the themes of submission and sacrificial service.

raised him from the dead" (LEB). He explains what kind of apostle he is by saying what kind he is *not*. This sets the stage for the issues he tackles later in the letter. In Philemon, the credential Paul chooses is "prisoner of Christ Jesus." In the letters to the Thessalonians, Paul just uses his name; no other credential is provided.

The letter to the Philippians is motivated by personal matters: reaffirming Paul's ties to Philippian believers, explaining the unplanned return of Epaphroditus, and weighing in on the dispute between Euodia and Syntyche. There are no matters of doctrine or ministry practice to correct. Thankfulness, submission, and self-sacrifice permeate the letter. Paul encourages the believers to follow his model as he follows Christ (see 3:17). Of all the possible credentials that Paul had available, he chooses only one.

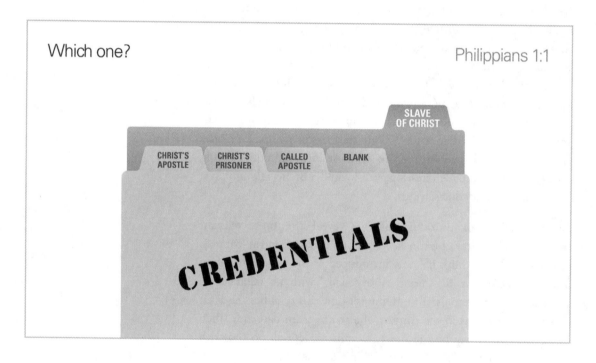

Does he choose apostle of Christ Jesus? Prisoner for Christ Jesus? Neither. He chooses "a slave of Christ Jesus" because it fits best with his objectives for the context. Think about how important obedience, humility, and submission are in the life of a slave or a servant. Proverbs 19:10 highlights the inappropriateness of a servant exercising authority over princes, whereas Proverbs 17:2 affirms the positive consequences of being a wise and faithful servant: ruling over the shameful son. These proverbs are not contradictory but complementary. The path to honor, esteem, and authority for a slave or servant is humble, faithful submission.

Likewise, Paul chooses "slave" as his credential because the qualities of a faithful servant mesh with his exhortations of the Philippians. He has willingly accepted his circumstances (imprisonment). He views them as ordained by God for the advancement of the gospel and exhorts the Philippians to adopt this perspective. Far from being a victim, Paul rejoices and will continue to rejoice in these circumstances. He'll unpack the key to this throughout the letter. But fundamentally it begins with a willing, thankful submission to God. The slave credential sets the stage for the exhortations and affirmations that follow.

There are three big ideas is this opening section: Paul's greeting extends "grace and peace" (1:2), he "gives thanks" for them in his prayers (1:3), and he is "content"—as he shows through his prayer for them (1:9). Paul's description of how he thanks God for the believers is one complex thought that stretches through 1:7. Let's take a look at each part.

Basis of Paul's Prayer: Paul utilizes a special device to signal that 1:6 is important. The reference to "this same thing" accomplishes the same attention-getting effect as saying, "Listen to *this*!" or "Guess *what*?" The italicized words refer to something important that follows. In this case, it is the assurance that God, the author and originator of life, will be faithful to complete the work He started. He will not abandon us.

Basis of Paul's Prayer   Philippians 1:6

Convinced of this same thing,

that He who began a good work in you will finish it until the day of Christ Jesus

Verse 5 describes the focus of Paul's thanksgiving: the Philippians' faithful partnership with him in his ministry of the gospel. Verse 6 elaborates on the big idea of giving thanks, providing a basis for doing so. Paul does several things here to frame how he wants the Philippians to understand their situation. "This same thing" refers ahead to a key idea—drawing more attention to it. The idea is that God finishes what He begins, including the good work in their lives (1:6).

But instead of calling Him "God," Paul uses "He who began a good work in you." The change from the standard "God" or "Lord" is risky because his audience has to figure out to whom Paul is referring. Paul is forcing us to think about God in a specific way—in this specific context. Paul has a reason for doing so.

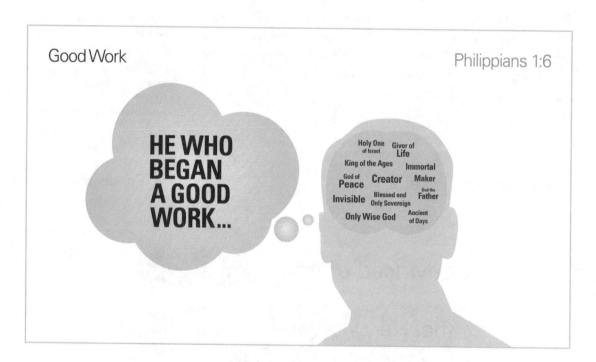

Think about all of the different qualities we might conjure up when God is mentioned. By using an expression other than the normal one, Paul forces us to think about the particular quality he highlights.

Despite the negative appearance of the circumstances, God is still in control and still accomplishing His purposes in the life of Paul and in our own lives. Beginning the "good work" was not a mistake that will be left incomplete. Adopting God's perspective on the situation requires us to give up our wrong perspectives. Paul affirms in 1:7 that this is the proper way to think about things, implying that the Philippians should think this way.

The final big idea of this section is introduced in 1:9, where Paul describes *what* he prays for the Philippians. Again, he uses a forward-pointing reference ("this" in NET, NIV, and NASB) to draw attention to his key idea.

His Prayer   Philippians 1:9–11

And this I pray:

that your love may abound
still more and more in knowledge and all discernment...

He prays that their love would abound, emphasizing "still more and more." This assumes a love is already present and focuses on its development. This love is grounded in knowledge and all discernment, not some warm, fuzzy feeling. To what end? Verse 10 provides the answer: "to be able to discern what is excellent in order to be sincere and blameless at Christ's return." Verse 11 elaborates on the idea of being sincere and blameless by describing what brings these things about. Being filled with the fruit of righteousness is the key. Lest we think that this fruit is something we can obtain through our own activity, Paul qualifies it as the kind that comes through Jesus Christ.

His Prayer: Paul highlights the content of his prayer using the same technique as in 1:6: a forward-pointing reference comparable to "Hey, get *this*!" in English. Paul's prayer for the Philippians is highlighted because it forms the big idea for this section of the letter.

Philippians 1:12–17

This section of the letter transitions from the introduction and preliminary statements to the reason Paul wrote this letter. In 1:12, Paul says that his circumstances in prison are actually advancing the gospel, not hindering it. But why would he say this? What issue is he addressing here? Paul's goal in this section is to change the Philippians' perspective on his circumstances. He wants them to see that what appears to be a bad thing is actually a good thing. Why? God is using it.

Paul is also going to ask them to do much more than just accept his perspective on the situation (see 4:29–30). What attitude is Paul addressing here? It has to do with having a *human* perspective on our circumstances instead of seeing things from *God's* perspective. This is not a problem unique to the Philippians or the early church; it is something we all struggle with. Here is a little background.

Frequently in the Psalms (and elsewhere as well) we find claims like this: The righteous are suffering, the wicked are prospering, and God isn't doing anything about it. This is the same sentiment that Paul addresses here regarding the Philippians' view of his own circumstances.

When you find yourself in dire straits without hope for change, it can foster a range of emotions. You might ask God: "How long?" or "Why have you forgotten me?" There may be outright anger and indignation. Such responses seem reasonable, especially in light of assurances like 1:6 that God will complete the good work He began in us. It is easy to feel distanced from God or abandoned when circumstances prevent us from doing something we feel called to do. In our prayers, we implore God to deliver us from our circumstances or to somehow change them. Where is God in such cases? Has He abandoned us? From the Philippians' perspective, Paul is supposed to be spreading the gospel. What could possibly be worse for this cause than being in prison?

If we allow our perspective toward the circumstances to prevail, it can make us utterly useless to God (see Psa 73:21–22). Frustration can turn to bitterness and hopelessness, making us completely ineffective. Something needs to change, but what?

In the Bible, what happens when God's people cry out to Him about the wicked prospering and the righteous falling? What changes? Not what you'd think. The vast majority of the time, it is the *attitude* about the circumstances that God changes rather than the circumstances themselves. The key is to see things from God's perspective instead of from our own human perspective. It is only then that we can find the hope, courage, and faith to move forward.

For this reason, Paul's primary purpose in this section is to change the Philippians' perspective of his circumstances. With this background, let's see how Paul goes about doing this.

Paul highlights the big idea for this section by saying, "I want you to know, brothers … ." Does he only want us to know what's in 1:12? These "I want you to know" statements highlight significant ideas—not just one idea. The same goes for referring to the Philippians as "brothers." (They already know he is addressing them, and he is *not* excluding the women here.) We do the same thing in English today. Picture a coach in a huddle. Midway through the pep talk, just before he gets to the key point, he says, "Alright people, I want you to …" or "Remember that …" We know the coach wouldn't be telling us something unimportant, so why say things like this? Why do pastors say things like "Don't miss this, people …" or "If you don't remember anything else folks, remember this …"? It's all about getting our attention. Since not everything is of equal importance, we use special markers to indicate what is especially important. Paul's "I want you to know" statement does the same thing.

Paul's statement also does something else: inserting this statement (especially in combination with "brothers" or "people") causes a *delay*. This disruption adds suspense. Paul and other New Testament writers use this strategy to make their big ideas stand out. Paul uses this method here because his big idea for this section is going to rock their view of the world. He's going to drop a theological bomb.

Paul's Circumstances   Philippians 1:12

ADVANCING THE
GOSPEL
NOT HOLDING
IT BACK

Philippians' Perspective

In 1:13, Paul elaborates on how his circumstances are a good thing. Word of his imprisonment has spread to everyone. Note that he singles out the imperial guard from "all the rest." If he had just said "all" or "everyone," there is a good chance that the imperial guard would not have come to mind. By specifically mentioning them and then adding "all the rest," he draws attention to this important group of witnesses.

Paul's Circumstances: The letter to the Philippians was written in part to address their concern for his circumstances in prison and its effect on his ministry. From their perspective, imprisonment meant a huge setback. Paul shatters this notion in 1:12, claiming that his circumstances actually served to advance the gospel rather than holding it back. Hearing this news would have been like dropping a theological bomb, destroying their flawed perspective about the situation.

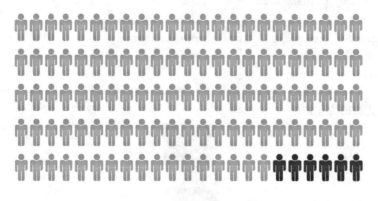

Singling Them Out

Philippians 1:13–14

All the rest, most of them   Imperial guards, believers

Singling Them Out: Twice in rapid succession Paul uses a device to single out a particular group of people for special consideration. Instead of simply saying that "all" had heard about Christ, he refers to the imperial guard "and all the rest." We often do the same kind of thing by saying something happened "in front of God and everyone," or "everyone and their brother was there." In both cases, we take an expression that is already comprehensive and add to it. In Paul's case, mentioning the guard draws attention to them, even though they are implicitly included. The effect is achieved by referring to "most" of the brothers. It makes us wonder, "What about the rest of them?" This sets the stage for Paul to talk about this minority group in 1:15–17.

Paul does the same kind of singling out again in 1:14 by talking about "most" of the believers rather than "all" of them. I could do the same kind of thing by saying I liked *most* of the sermon or that I *mostly* liked you as a friend. Chances are you'd be wondering which part I *didn't* like. This is exactly what Paul is doing here. In 1:15 and 17 he is going to talk about this unnamed subgroup of believers. It seems that not everyone who was preaching was doing so out of pure motives.

The first group of evangelists (mentioned in 1:15) are those preaching because of envy or strife; more detail will be given about them in 1:17. This negative group is contrasted with a positive group. Paul highlights the distinctions that separate the two. At the beginning of 1:15, the Greek word "men," typically untranslated, let the original audience know that Paul was also going to address a second group that was preaching for the right reasons.

In English, it would be like Paul saying, "While some preach out of envy and strife … ." Including "while" or "although" helps us lean forward a bit and pay attention to the second part—typically the more important of the two. Paul highlights the contrast with "envy" and "strife" by emphasizing "goodwill" in the Greek.

The contrast of these two groups continues in 1:16–17, including elaboration about the motivation of each. Those who preach out of love do so because they have recognized Paul's role; he was appointed "for the defense of the gospel" (emphasized in Greek). He wants the Philippians to know that his imprisonment has not changed this. He wants them to respond like the majority of believers, those who have been encouraged to preach. Emphasis drives home the contrast, stressing that the minority preach out of "rivalry" and "not sincerely." Stating the same thing both positively and negatively adds further reinforcement. How could their preaching be based on ambition and rivalry? The elaboration makes it clear: They intend to cause distress and affliction to Paul by adding to the frustration of his circumstances.

Counterpoint/Point: Paul draws a series of contrasts between two groups of people in 1:15–17: the majority and those remaining few that he singles out in 1:14. Using an "on the one hand/on the other" style, Paul contrasts their motives and their rationale for proclaiming the Gospel. These conflicting factors likely troubled the Philippians, but Paul addresses the issue head on. He is getting them ready for a different perspective—what he's going to say in the rest of the letter (see 1:18).

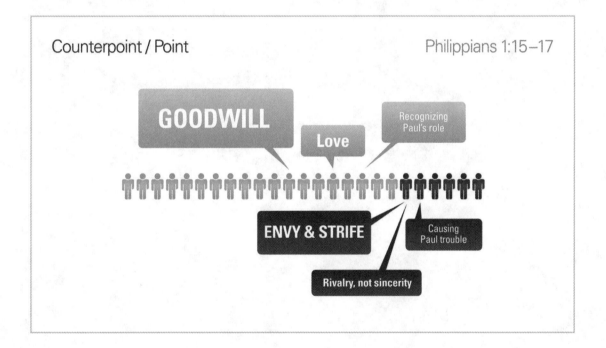

From the Philippians' perspective—a human perspective—all hope seems lost for the advancement of the gospel because of Paul's imprisonment. His ministry appears derailed. This is the perspective that Paul is actively working to change. Jesus' call to deny ourselves, take up our cross, and follow Him sounds simple on Sunday morning. Yet it is very difficult to practice—especially when we contend with adverse circumstances: pain, turmoil, and tests. When we feel as though God has forgotten or ignored our plight, we have to make a decision. Will we trust in our own perspective, or trust that God will really do what He has promised? Paul chose God's perspective and urged the Philippians to do the same! He claims that far from stifling the gospel, his imprisonment is actually advancing it. This claim forms the big idea of the next sections in 1:18–26.

Philippians 1:18–20

Most translations begin this section with "What then?" But the Greek marker *gar* ("for") indicates that it is intended to strengthen or support what precedes—namely, his last big idea. This question in 1:18 is rhetorical, constraining us to pause and think about the implications of his last big idea. How is it that imprisonment can be a good thing for the gospel? Paul gives us the answer in 1:18.

How are they preaching? Paul has just contrasted two groups who preach the gospel for very different reasons. From the Philippians' standpoint, this sounds like a horrible thing. Paul seeks to change their view by helping them consider the outcome. No matter what the means or motive, Christ is being proclaimed. Yogi Berra used to say when giving directions to his house, "When you come to the fork in the road, take it!" This was not mystical advice. Both paths lead to the same destination. Even though it may have been better to preach with right motives, Paul urged the believers not to forget the outcome in either case: Christ is proclaimed.

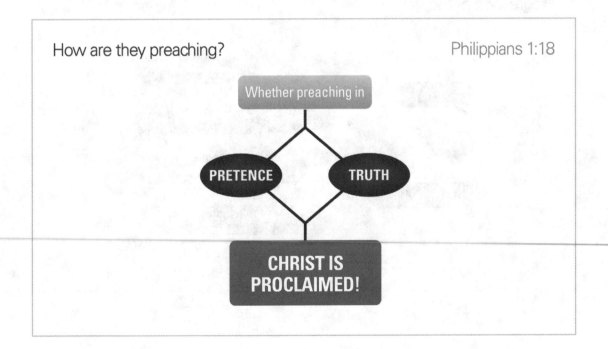

How are they preaching?   Philippians 1:18

Whether preaching in

PRETENCE   TRUTH

CHRIST IS PROCLAIMED!

No matter why people might be preaching, they are still preaching. It is a no-lose proposition. When Yogi Berra used to tell people coming to his house, "When you come to the fork in the road, take it," he was not joking; *both* paths eventually lead to the same spot. This is essentially the same point that Paul makes here. Christ is being proclaimed, regardless of motive. While it would be better for everyone to preach with right motives, we must not lose sight of the big picture: The gospel is spreading. In Paul's case, this would happen with or without his freedom.

This raises the next question. If Paul's circumstances are actually *advancing* the gospel rather than hindering it, now what? How should he or the Philippians respond? Rather than fretting over the competing motivations for preaching, what does Paul do? He chooses to rejoice over the results. Christ is being proclaimed, so why shouldn't he rejoice? It is important to track his progression of thought through this section. Each thought or question leads into the next one.

Progression of Thought: Paul traces a complex thread through this section, adding one "for" statement on top of another. Each statement serves to strengthen and support the one that precedes. It's very much like answering a series of "why" questions in a dialogue. Paul accomplishes the same task, but in the form of a monologue using the "for" statements.

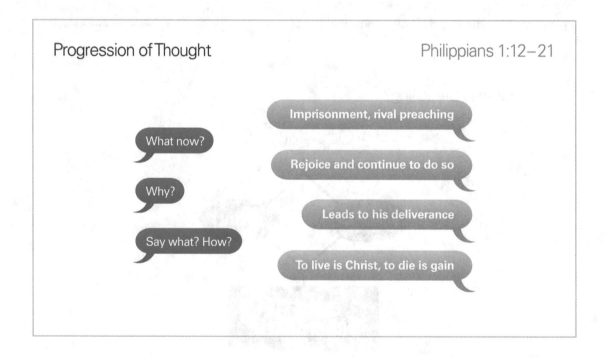

Progression of Thought   Philippians 1:12–21

What now?   Imprisonment, rival preaching

Why?   Rejoice and continue to do so

                   Leads to his deliverance

Say what? How?   To live is Christ, to die is gain

Twice in 1:18 Paul claims that he rejoices over the advance of the gospel. The first statement describes his response to the current state of the gospel. Regardless of how or why the gospel is advancing, Paul chooses to rejoice rather than grumble or be discouraged. Rejoicing is a choice; it's not the natural response we'd expect. The second statement concerns the prospects for the future. His decision to rejoice now is not something that will pass away but something he will endeavor to continue.

The last part of 1:18 actually corrects Paul's first claim about rejoicing. Why? If he had only said, "I rejoice," it would have opened the possibility that he would not continue to do so. If he had only stated that he *will* rejoice, it could have been viewed as though he were waiting for some kind of change to come about first. You could paraphrase the sentiment by saying, "In this, I rejoice. As a matter of fact, I'll even continue to do so." The word for "even" in Greek makes it sound as if rejoicing is the least likely possibility. He's not just rejoicing—he will even continue to do so.

Choice to Rejoice: In 1:18, Paul states the same thing twice, but there is a bit more going on here than appears. His first statement about rejoicing is "replaced" in Greek by the affirmation that he will rejoice. It is phrased as though the first statement was somehow in need of correction. He could have simply said one or the other, or he could have added one to the other, but instead he replaces the first. There is another Greek word in the second statement that makes it sound like the commitment to rejoicing is the least likely thing one might do. He's not just rejoicing now, he's even going to continue to do so.

Choice to Rejoice   Philippians 1:18

I will rejoice!

~~I rejoice!~~

To rejoice you have to do more than just accept your circumstances. You have to trust and be thankful. The trust is based on the character of the one who began the good work (1:6). It is trust in the faithfulness which He has shown. For Paul, this meant trusting God because He chose him—an unlikely leader of the early church—to be an apostle. Without trust, what else would Paul cling to? Nothing. Too often our trust in the Lord is based on *our own* understanding, or only engages *part* of our heart (see Prov 3:5–6). When the storms of life come, faulty foundations are destroyed. What we need to do is trust the Lord with *all* of our heart and not lean on *our own* understanding.

One of the greatest litmus tests for trust is thanksgiving, a theme that resonates throughout Philippians. If I'm afraid of my situation or grumbling about it, then chances are I'm leaning on my own understanding. This same perspective leads me to say my situation is wrong, unfair, or needs to change. If I'm really trusting God to be in control of all things, then this will be reflected in my perspective. I may not like my predicament, but I can still choose to trust God to accomplish His purposes no matter how dire things get. My choice to trust in God's character enables me to give thanks for His provision even though it is not what I would choose.

How does Paul respond to his situation? He rejoices, and better yet, he'll continue to rejoice. We learned in our discussion of 1:12 that in Scripture, *perspectives* about circumstances are changed more often than the circumstances themselves. We see the same thing with Paul and his imprisonment. By telling the Philippians his perspective and his positive response to his circumstances, he is challenging them to adopt a similar response. He does this because he knows he has been appointed for the defense of the gospel (see 1:15). Changes in circumstances don't affect this.

It is one thing to verbally affirm your calling, and quite another to live your life in light of it—to view your circumstances through this lens. We have all had a number of "dark nights of the soul" that pushed us to question our calling. Doubts creep in, especially when people are critical or circumstances look bleak. When we lose sight of the big picture, it's easy to get discouraged. But as we follow God and keep in step with His plan for our lives, we can confidently trust that the one who began the good work in us will indeed complete it (see 1:6). God is not just the creator of all things, He is the finisher of what He has started.

So what is the bigger picture that enables Paul to look beyond his circumstances and rejoice? It is his confidence that these things will turn out for his deliverance (1:19). This confidence is based on two things: the prayers of the Philippians and the support of the Holy Spirit.

One of the key things that helps me through difficult times is the body of Christ, the church. At several critical junctures in my life, people whom I trusted and respected let me know they were praying for me. Some of them even asked what they could be praying about specifically. It is encouraging to know that I'm not standing alone. The problem is that more and more these days we isolate ourselves from one another rather than share our lives. Even though Paul was physically separated from the Philippians, he made his life an open book to them through this letter. Sharing our lives with other believers is vital to a vibrant spiritual life. It enables us to bear one another's burdens. But there is another even more important component needed.

That other needed element is a close relationship with the author and perfector of our faith through the indwelling of His Spirit. People will let us down eventually; no one is perfect but God alone. The support of the Spirit doesn't just include His ministry within us; it is often manifested in His ministering through other people. Remember the people I mentioned that provided encouragement to me? Why did they do it? In most cases, it was in response to a prompting of the Spirit, sensing they should give me a call or ask how I was doing. This is what people are referring to when they talk about "divine appointments"—seemingly chance encounters that have a huge effect. But you can only be prompted by the Spirit and ministered to if you are in relationship with Him. How do we keep that relationship current and vibrant? By spending time in prayer, meditating on God's Word, and regularly confessing our sin. Neglecting any one of these will encumber His ministry in our lives and our ability to minister to others.

Paul elaborates in 1:20 about why he is confident that he will be delivered. At first, we might think that deliverance for Paul means release from prison. But Paul unfurls a wholly different set of values than what we might expect. Paul states, "I know that …" in 1:19, describing his confidence in his deliverance. A second thing that he knows is provided in 1:20.

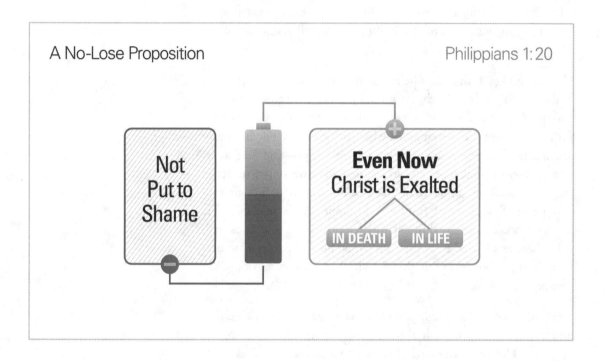

A No-Lose Proposition   Philippians 1:20

Not Put to Shame

Even Now
Christ is Exalted

IN DEATH   IN LIFE

A No-Lose Proposition: Just as in 1:18, Paul points out that no matter what the outcome, Christ is exalted. The Philippians were concerned for Paul's welfare in prison, fearing the worst. He showed them that the advancement of the gospel did not depend on the motivation of those preaching. Here he claims that the same holds true for his present situation. Whether he remains alive and productive or whether he is executed in prison, two things are guaranteed to happen. He will *not* be put to shame, and Christ will be exalted in him. These things are not contingent upon his life or death, his freedom or imprisonment.

He states what he knows both negatively and positively to emphasize his point. He knows that "in nothing" will he be put to shame. Instead of shame, Christ will be exalted in him "even now," as always. One way or the other, this exaltation will come about—through life or death.

Paul casts this as a no-lose proposition. If his comfort or physical deliverance from imprisonment is the standard against which things are measured, his prospects indeed look bleak. Being appointed for the defense of the gospel (1:16) did not come with a safety guarantee. Despite the peril of imprisonment, the situation has actually helped advance his cause rather than hinder it. If exalting Christ becomes our basis of evaluation instead of comfort or security, what we value radically changes. Paul's faith is not just a set of closely held beliefs. It is unmistakably reflected in the value judgments he makes, which he describes in more detail in 1:21–26.

Philippians 1:21–26

At the close of the last section Paul made an audacious statement. He said that it really didn't matter whether he lived or died; either way Christ would be exalted in him. Talk about a change in perspective! If seeing Christ exalted really was the most important thing in our lives, how would that change our priorities and perspective? What would it do to our outlook for the future? This section tackles these questions. It focuses on the practical implications of life and death, aside from what we think or feel.

The big idea for this section is: "to live is Christ and to die is gain." The NET Bible translates the two options as "living" and "dying." The "for" in the phrase "For to me" signals that what follows strengthens and supports his assertion at the end of 1:20. How can Paul say that Christ will be exalted either in his life or death? Living means continued work for Christ, and dying means going to be with Him. The simplicity with which Paul treats life-and-death issues casts things in a whole new light. "To me" indicates that Paul's values system reflects his own perspective on the matter, but by implication it is one that we should adopt as well.

This section is essentially a pro/con list, cataloging the advantages and disadvantages of living versus dying.

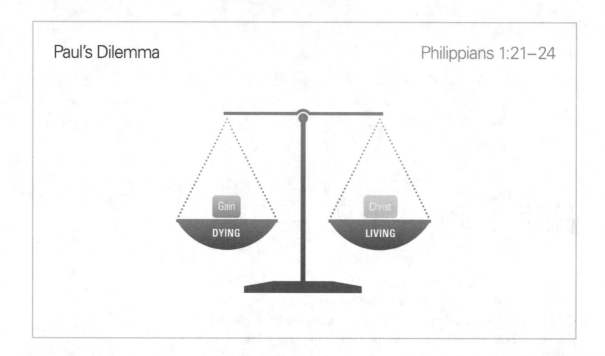

Paul's Dilemma   Philippians 1:21–24

Gain — DYING   Christ — LIVING

Paul's Dilemma: In 1:21–24, Paul gives us insight into how he weighs out the options before him: living versus dying. Since Christ is glorified in him in either case, and since the gospel is advancing whether he is free to participate or not, should he stay or should he go?

He could have simply told us his choice, but instead he walks us through his decision-making process. He takes up the first option of living in 1:22, qualifying it as "in the flesh." This ensures us that he is talking about his present life and not about living in a glorified body after physical death. His continued ministry in this present life means fruitful work for Christ—a bonus for the believers to whom he is ministering (see 1:24).

At the end of 1:22 and into verse 23, Paul makes clear that this is no easy decision. Why is it so hard? Because *life* is hard! The prospect of departing from the pain, suffering, and hardship of earthly life in order to be with Christ is clearly better. Who wouldn't want to be in the heaven described in Revelation 7:16–17—a place where there is no longer hunger or thirst, where God Himself will wipe away every tear from our eyes? To Paul the prospect of heaven must have sounded even better. Five times he received thirty-nine lashes, three times he was beaten with rods and shipwrecked, and he was even stoned once (see 2 Cor 11:23–29)! He knew hardship. If anyone deserved a break, it was Paul. It's no wonder leaving this life to be with Christ had a certain appeal, but there are other considerations to take into account.

Paul's Dilemma: Based on the first pair of factors considered, dying sounds like the better option. He would no longer have to be in pain or suffer imprisonment, nor would he have to deal with problems in the church. It would not be his problem anymore. On the other hand, remaining means more fruitful labor for Christ. Which will he choose? At this point, it sounds like he is leaning toward departing as the better thing.

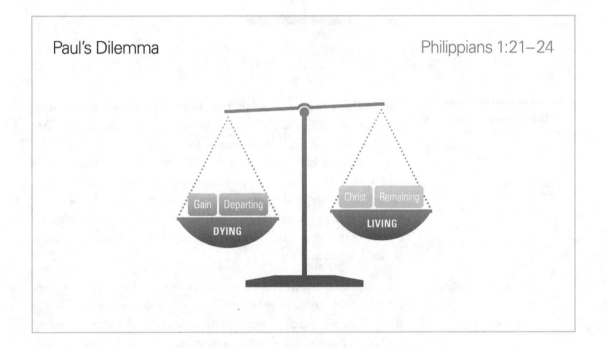

Paul's Dilemma — Philippians 1:21–24

Gain | Departing — DYING

Christ | Remaining — LIVING

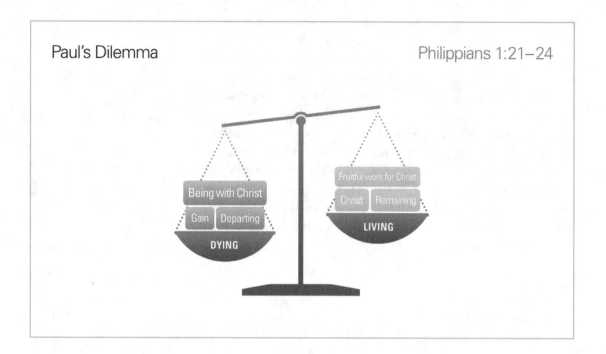

Paul's Dilemma — Philippians 1:21–24

Paul's Dilemma: Despite the potential for fruitful work if he remains, departing and being with Christ has its appeal. After all, if Christ is exalted in either case, if the gospel advances with or without him, why not be with the Lord?

These other considerations are raised in 1:24. He mentioned earlier that remaining in the flesh and ministering would be fruitful. He uses the same "in the flesh" terminology to tie back to 1:22, but states that remaining is *not* just about fruitfulness—it is necessary for the Philippians' sake. Just as his imprisonment was of less concern than the advancement of the gospel (see 1:18), teaching the Philippians is higher priority than going to be with Christ. Their needs are what tip the scales in favor of remaining in the flesh. What is most desirable for Paul is secondary.

After listing the pros and cons of each option, Paul makes known his choice. He could have skipped comparing the options, but doing so would have obscured the significance of his decision. Opening up his decision-making process challenges us to follow in his path. How do we decide to get involved in a ministry or not, to minister to someone else's needs or not? Do we consider only our own interests? What about the interests of others (see 2:4)? Convinced that the Philippians' needs outweigh his own desire to depart and be with Christ, Paul chooses to remain serving them.

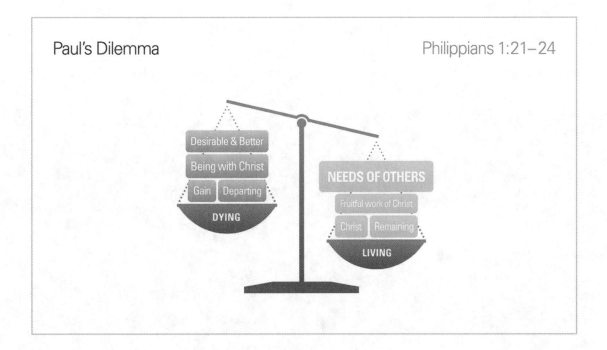

The idea of remaining is essentially stated twice in the Greek, with the second reference adding the sense of continuing to live and serve. He remains because of their progress; for Paul, joy in the faith is top priority. To what end? Paul uses a somewhat cryptic catch-all—"that which they may be proud of"—to describe what he wants to see increase. In light of the preceding reference to progress and joy in the faith, what he wants to see is their confident growth in Christ. This will be a result of him remaining in the flesh. More specifically, he wants to return to the Philippian church to work with them directly.

In the next chapter, Paul tells us that we need to balance looking out for our needs with considering the needs of others. The focus of the current section is on weighing our decisions: Are they based on our own comfort, or are they a ministry to others? The lure of gratifying the flesh, even in non-sinful ways, can distract us from choosing something better. I cannot remember a time where I received more spiritual fulfillment from lying on the couch than from helping meet someone else's need. Though there are practical limits to how much of ourselves we can give away before we burn out (see 2:4), seeing Paul's version of a pro/con list raises the bar for what it means to serve.

Paul's Dilemma: Even though departing and being with Christ is desirable and better, Paul chooses a different path. In keeping with the broader theme of this book, Paul uses the more attractive option of departing as a backdrop for disclosing his decision to remain and serve the church. Had he jumped ahead to deliver his final verdict without weighing out the options, we would not understand what it cost him. Departing from his circumstances and being with Christ, while desirable, would have been selfish on his part. Instead, he opts for the same kind of sacrificial service that we will read about Christ offering in 2:5–11.

Philippians 1:27–30

This section of Philippians is connected to the last section, where Paul announced his decision to remain in the flesh to serve the believers rather than depart to be with the Lord. He did not condition his decision on anything, but beginning the first sentence with "only" is about as close as one can get. My mom used to tell me I could do anything I wanted while she was out—*only* I needed to get the dishes done and finish my homework. In reality, I couldn't do *anything*; I could do what fit into the leftover time. The "only" statement placed constraints on what sounded like an open-ended arrangement. In the same way, Paul's offer to remain in the flesh comes with an obligation on the Philippians' part.

If Paul is indeed going to remain, then the Philippians are expected to live in a certain manner—one that is "worthy of the gospel" (emphasized in Greek). Why should they do this? So that he could hear about "the things" concerning them, and perhaps even see them. Most translations smooth over this extra reference by omitting it, but it serves an important purpose. "The things concerning you" is a reference that attracts attention to "standing firm in one spirit." When he mentions "the things," it would have made the original audience listen more closely to see exactly *which things* he meant.

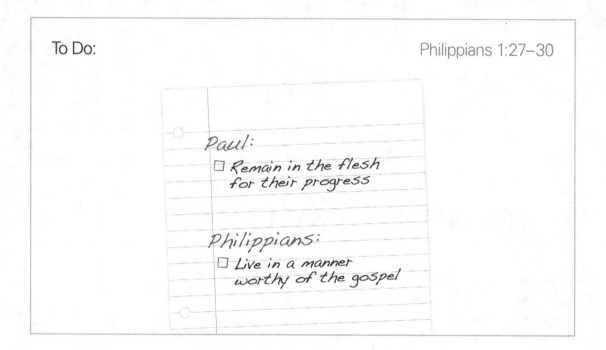

Paul:
☐ Remain in the flesh for their progress

Philippians:
☐ Live in a manner worthy of the gospel

To Do: Paul's decision to remain and serve the church was not conditioned on anything; he decided to put the Philippians' interests before his own. But if remaining was on Paul's to-do list, then the Philippians must understand what he expected them to do in return. His expectation is reflected in the use of "only" at the beginning of 1:27. Imagine me saying you can do anything you want … only be sure to do [fill in the blank]. It effectively narrows down what sounded like an unconditional commitment to remain on earth. If he had made this a condition for his remaining, the believers could potentially have opted out. By deciding to stay and then describing his expectations for them, Paul leaves them little room to do otherwise.

What does it practically look like to stand firm in one spirit? Paul elaborates on this by providing both a positive and a negative component. The positive part is contending for the faith—and not just in any old way. He wants them to contend "with one mind"—not every person for themselves. Even the action of "striving" (ESV) includes the idea of unity. It could be more literally translated as "doing something side by side" (see LEB).

The negative part correlates with the positive part and has to do with how we respond to opponents. Adversaries will come from outside and within the faith. It should not come as a surprise that we'll face opposition to the gospel, even if it doesn't entail imprisonment like Paul faced. The key question is: How will we respond when it comes? Will we be alarmed and cower? Will we allow ourselves to be intimidated? Since we know that opposition is inevitable, it's critical to decide how we will respond *now*, before our backs are pressed against the wall.

We can't just strive for the faith and cower before opposition. We can't just hunker down against resistance without moving forward. *Both* are necessary components.

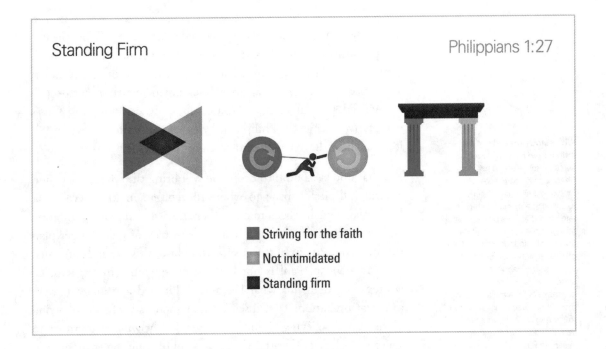

Standing Firm   Philippians 1:27

- Striving for the faith
- Not intimidated
- Standing firm

Elaborating on both the positive and negative aspects of what it takes to stand firm corrects our expectations about what lies ahead and enables us to prepare for it now.

There is a brief aside in 1:28 that provides God's perspective on the matter of striving for the faith and facing opposition. Opposition can cause us to second-guess our decisions: Should we have done this? Was it all a mistake? If I had done it differently, would things have gone more smoothly? To address these issues, Paul reframes *striving for something* in the face of opposition. How do you deal with the doubts and second-guessing? By going back to what you know to be true. If God has really called them to this ministry, and if opposition is to be expected as a natural consequence of its message, then why doubt? They doubt because they're relying on their own perspective. Paul addresses this once again by recasting things from God's perspective.

The Philippian church's struggle is a sign of destruction to their opponents. But God will triumph in the end—putting their opponents on the losing side. Paul wants the Philippian church to think of their struggle as a sign of salvation. This is for the same reason

Standing Firm: Paul describes striving for the faith as having two parts. Both must be present for us to be effective. It involves *doing* one thing while *avoiding* doing something else—creating a positive/negative opposition. The positive aspect is contending for the faith with a united spirit. The negative aspect is avoiding being intimidated by those opposing the gospel. We shouldn't neglect either part.

that Paul said in 1:19–20 that the opposition he faced would lead to deliverance and salvation (same Greek word as in 1:28). Recall the no-lose proposition he outlined in 1:20. This same principle applies here. Everything happening is from God (end of 1:28). Nothing comes as a surprise to Him. Here again it boils down to whose perspective we will adopt: our own or God's. Not only can adopting God's perspective change the Philippians' view of Paul's situation (1:12–18), it affects how they view their own circumstances (1:27–28).

Paul has one last bomb to drop. He will bring the whole discussion around full circle—back to where they began in 1:12. Recall that Paul's main goal has been to make them understand that his suffering and imprisonment are not a mistake, but part of God's larger plan for the advancement of the gospel. In light of this, he adds one final piece in 1:29–30. Paul is not looking for empathy from them; he is preparing them for what lies ahead. Phrased as though it were a special invitation, Paul discloses that there is more to following Christ than believing. It has been graciously *granted* to them to suffer on behalf of Christ—the same kind of suffering that Paul has experienced and is presently experiencing.

Why stand firm and not be intimidated? Paul has laid some pretty heavy truths on the Philippians in this chapter. So far though, all of the references to suffering and sacrifice have referred to Paul. He now turns the tables on them, saying that these things apply to them as well. Paul phrases it as he would an invitation to something desirable. To be sure, believing in Christ is indeed desirable, but there is something more. It has also been appointed to them to suffer. In what manner? Verse 30 discloses that they will suffer like Paul has.

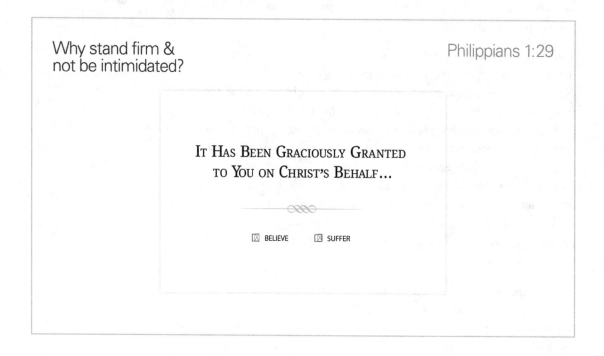

Why stand firm & not be intimidated?

Philippians 1:29

IT HAS BEEN GRACIOUSLY GRANTED TO YOU ON CHRIST'S BEHALF...

☒ BELIEVE   ☒ SUFFER

The word translated as *granted* is more often used in the context of forgiveness, sharing the same basic root as *grace*. It is also used to describe granting something positive, as in 2:9, where Jesus is given a name above all others. So why phrase it this way? From a human perspective, not many people want to suffer. Suffering is often viewed more as a burden to bear than as a gift to cherish. Phrased as it is, Paul presents suffering as a special thing graciously granted by God. It's like the difference between an invitation saying, "Come on over!" and one that reads, "We graciously request the pleasure of your presence."

This is much more than marketing; it has to do with a change of perspective. As long as we insist on viewing the world through our own perspective—with comfort, security, and happiness as the benchmark—we will never accomplish what God desires. For Paul, the key is exchanging our view for God's. Paul processes his circumstances through God's perspective, and he challenges the Philippians to do the same. We shouldn't just accept the fact that we may suffer for Christ; we should embrace it.

Philippians 2

Philippians 2:1–4

I was teaching through Philippians when a woman asked, "Which 'if' is this in 2:1—the one that means 'if' or the one that means 'since'?" In other words, if all of these "if" statements are true, why not use "since" instead? After thinking about it for a moment, it became clear that Paul knew exactly what he was doing. He was drawing attention to his big idea.

Since Paul was using a Greek convention, I wondered how we would accomplish the same thing in English. What if Paul had reframed the conditions as yes/no questions? Would that have the same effect? Take a look:

Is there any encouragement in Christ? (Well, yes, I suppose there is.)

Is there any consolation of love? (Well, yes, I guess so.)

Is there any fellowship of the Spirit? (Ok, that too.)

Is there any affection and compassion? (Yes, I suppose so.)

Big Idea: If all of these things are true, then complete my joy by agreeing!

Paul's goal was not to make us question these things, but to *remind* us that they are present.

This passage reminds me of how my dad used to ask me questions about "what I knew to be true" as a means of correcting me. He would work me into a corner using obvious questions that challenged me to reconcile my (negative) behavior with what I claimed to be true:

Do you love your sister? (Well, yes.)

Do you want her to be kind to you? (Yes, I suppose I do.)

Big Idea: If so, then ...

Framing true statements in the form of conditions has the same effect. By framing 2:1 in this way, Paul leaves the reader with no choice but to accept what follows.

Agree! All of these true "if" statements effectively lead the reader down a path that ends with no option but to positively respond to the "then" statement. Paul's argument funnels people toward his preferred response: being like-minded.

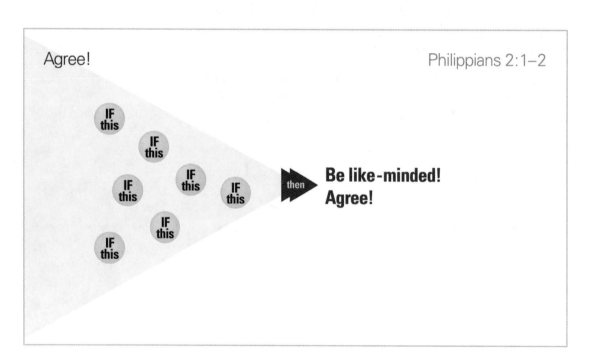

The command in 2:2 to "complete my joy" functions as a meta-comment—it's a comment on what he is about to say. Statements like "I don't want you to miss this!" do the same thing, where "this" refers to an important idea coming up. The meta-comment is another way that Paul highlights the big idea of the passage: that we should "be in agreement."

If indeed encouragement, consolation, and fellowship can be found in Christ, then why can't Christians get along with each other? It's because we have forgotten the things that make Christian unity possible. The statements in 2:2b–4 spell out what it (practically) looks like to agree. The elaborations give us real-life insight into what it takes to get along—with unity of love, spirit, and purpose being the key.

Same Mind: There is only one main verb in these verses; all of the others are secondary participles, elaborating on the one command to be like-minded. Because it is awkward in English to have so many elaborations in a row, most translations render the actions in 2:3–4 as main verbs, as commands. Regardless of how we translate it, the important thing to remember is that there is still only one big idea. The others are still important, but they play a supporting role.

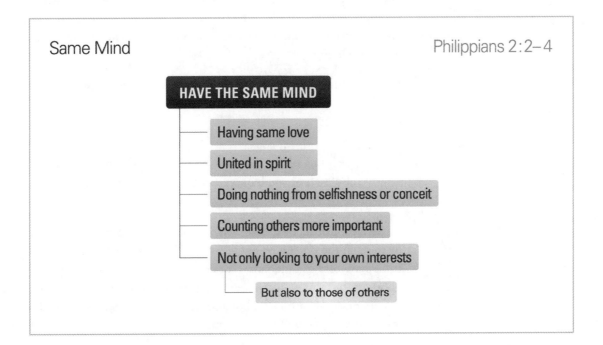

Same Mind   Philippians 2:2–4

HAVE THE SAME MIND
- Having same love
- United in spirit
- Doing nothing from selfishness or conceit
- Counting others more important
- Not only looking to your own interests
  - But also to those of others

The actions in 2:3–4 are secondary in Greek, even though most translations render them as though they were main actions, or commands. This tells us that Paul had one main idea; the other thoughts described what his main idea looked like in practice. Paul has one big idea: being like-minded. The other ideas are what bring it about.

There are two sets of paired statements in 2:3–4, each telling us what *not* to do before telling us what we *should* do. Normally the negative *follows* the positive. Telling us what *not* to do forces us to think about what we *should* do. This gives the positive alternative extra attention. Paul is highlighting something for us. Here is a paraphrase:

> Don't do anything from selfishness or conceit; instead, count others more important. Don't just look out for your own interests but the interests of others also (2:3–4).

Paul could have just told them to "work harder at considering one another's needs" and to "look out for the interests of others," without any negative counterpart. Using this negative/positive order rhetorically attracts our attention to what he thought was most important!

Verse 4 focuses on something more practical: looking out for other people's interests. The little word "also" plays a very significant role here:

> Each one of you not looking out for his own interests, but also each of you looking out for the interests of others.

At first glance, it looks like Paul is telling us to forsake our own interests in the pursuit of serving others, but this is not the case. He could have told us to look out for our own interests *and* the interests of others, but this would have made them equally important. Using the rhetorical "Not only … but also …" construction tells us that he wants us to do *both*. But there is more to it.

Paul uses the same negative/positive order he used in 2:3 to draw attention to his second statement. This statement is even more important than the last. Here's why: As selfish human beings, we most likely look out for our own interests, possibly even to the *exclusion* of anyone else's! The challenge is to do the one without ignoring the other. If we don't look after our own interests, we may burn out or be taken advantage of. Ignoring the interests of others would contradict the clear teaching of Scripture.

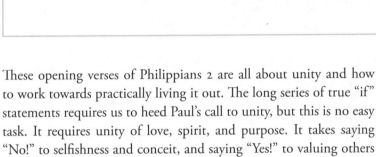

Like-Minded

YOUR INTERESTS

LIKE-MINDED AGREEMENT!

OTHERS' INTERESTS

These opening verses of Philippians 2 are all about unity and how to work towards practically living it out. The long series of true "if" statements requires us to heed Paul's call to unity, but this is no easy task. It requires unity of love, spirit, and purpose. It takes saying "No!" to selfishness and conceit, and saying "Yes!" to valuing others more than ourselves. Verse 4 provides balance, reminding us that valuing others is not to be done to the detriment of our own interests.

Living in like-minded unity—even with those we love—can be real work at times. Paul challenges us to reconcile our actions with what we say we believe. He also practically spells out the actions that bring about unity. Remember, the great blessings of consolation, affection, fellowship, and compassion that can be found in Christ are by-products of like-minded unity. We can experience these things if we heed Paul's exhortation to get along.

Like-Minded! It is not just a matter of your interests or those of others. Instead, we need to look out for the one without letting go of the other. Only then will a biblically-sound balance be struck. Looking only to our own interests results in selfishness. Looking only to the interests of others is not sustainable, even though it sounds like a good thing. The key is to do both.

Philippians 2:5–11

This section develops the big idea from the previous section about being like-minded. Even though 2:5–11 provides important theological commentary about Jesus, it has been placed here for a specific reason. In the context, the model of Jesus' humility and sacrifice is intended to reinforce Paul's call to consider others as being more important than ourselves. And what better example could there be than Jesus? Let's take a look at the traits of Jesus that are highlighted.

Paul connects this section to the previous one by asking us to think like Jesus did. He reminds us in 2:6 that Jesus is fully God, with all the rights and privileges that go with that. All that follows is to be understood in this context—namely, that Jesus has the form of God. His divine status provides the backdrop against which we should consider His example. So what does Jesus do with all this power and authority? Even though He was entitled to these things, Jesus does not use them to His own advantage. He does not consider equality with God as something to fight for or hold onto.

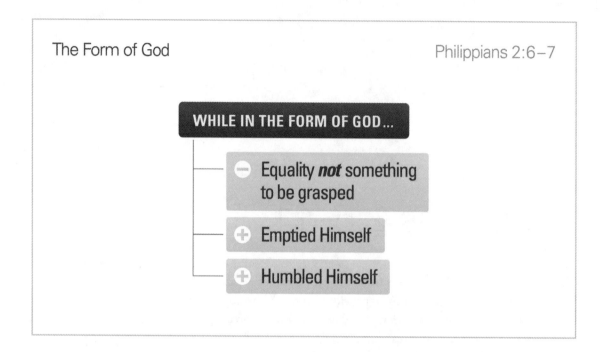

WHILE IN THE FORM OF GOD...

- Equality *not* something to be grasped

+ Emptied Himself

+ Humbled Himself

The Form of God: Jesus' decision to humble Himself and die on the cross took place in a specific context: while He was fully God. Instead of holding on to His "rights and privileges," He chose a different path. This path is described by Paul in both positive and negative terms. Even though He could have asserted His divine right, He chose instead not to regard equality with God as something to be grasped. On the contrary, He emptied and humbled Himself. The implication is that if Jesus is willing to set aside His own rights in obedience to the Father's higher purposes, then why can't we do the same? Why can't we be like-minded and consider others more important than ourselves?

Even though Jesus had the divine clout to do anything He wanted, He chose *not* to stick up for His rights.

What Jesus *did* is highlighted by the contrast with what He did *not* do. Paul follows this with two statements about what He *did* do. Instead of clinging on to His entitlements, He emptied Himself. How? By taking the form of a servant and the likeness of human form. This is where it gets exciting.

Think about it. Nearly every superhero I read about as a kid had two qualities. First, they had a human form, like Superman, Batman, or Spiderman. But there was also that thing that made them different. They also had some kind of special power that other humans didn't have. The same characteristics held true for the villains. They too had a human form and some special power. The thing that separated the good guys from the bad guys was what each did with their powers. The villains used their power to try to take over the world, while the heroes used theirs to fight for truth and justice. How does this relate to Philippians? Well, Jesus is in the same kind of position: fully human, yet still having His divine attributes. It raises the question of what Jesus will do with all that He has.

To build up the suspense before the answer, Paul slows things down at the end of 2:7 by nearly repeating his previous statement about Jesus being in human likeness. We do the same kind of thing before the peak of a story: "So there I am on the roof, sitting in my chair. While I'm sitting there … ."

We would naturally expect that whatever comes next is of significance to the story. This represents an intentional slowing, but not every translation represents this very well. There's even some controversy about where to divide the verse. The Greek slows down right before 2:8.

So the big question is: What is the significant thing that follows the repetition? It's what Jesus does with all His power and authority: He chooses to *humble* Himself instead of using His divine power to assert Himself. Paul elaborates on this in 2:8.

Humbled Himself: Paul draws attention to Jesus' response by repeating the same information. We often do the same thing in conversation: "I was looking out the window, minding my own business. But while I was looking out the window … ." Chances are you'd be disappointed if something significant did not follow. Paul lists two things that Jesus does, but the second is the more significant of the two. Each one is elaborated on using a secondary thought, practically describing what each action involves. Christ emptying Himself means He took on the form of a servant—He took on human likeness. What does humbling Himself look like, practically speaking? It looks like obedience to the most unthinkable, cruel kind of death—crucifixion.

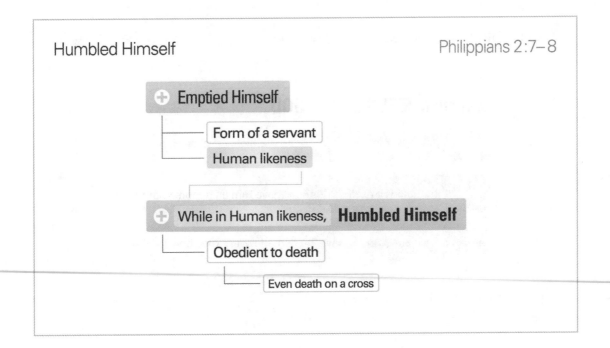

Humbled Himself   Philippians 2:7–8

- ⊕ **Emptied Himself**
  - Form of a servant
  - Human likeness
- ⊕ While in Human likeness, **Humbled Himself**
  - Obedient to death
    - Even death on a cross

He tells us that Jesus was obedient to death. We joke about doing things "to death," but this is the real deal! The implication is that He could not have been any more humbled or obedient. Why? Because He did much more than just suffer death. He did it in the most painful and humiliating manner: crucifixion.

Our human view of power and rights is tarnished by our sinful nature. Who hasn't been taken advantage of or trampled on at some point in their life? When we have power and rights granted to us, we're reluctant to give them up. Why? Because we're afraid that they will be used against us, leaving us in a position of weakness. Although this might describe how things work in our human context, it is not how God works.

What was the result of Christ's humiliation? Was it worth all of the pain, suffering, and hardship? Far from being taken advantage of, Christ is exalted in ways so wonderful that only God could have thought them up.

A Case-Study in Submission:
This passage contains some of the richest theology about Jesus' incarnation. Paul offers Jesus as the model of what it means to humble oneself and consider others more important. In God's economy of things, such a choice leads to honor and exaltation. This stands in stark contrast with our human perspective, which is exactly why Paul includes Jesus' example. It provides practical motivation to follow His lead.

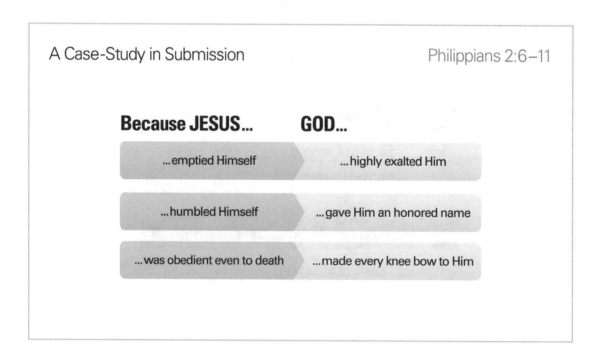

A Case-Study in Submission   Philippians 2:6–11

Because JESUS...   **GOD...**

...emptied Himself   ...highly exalted Him

...humbled Himself   ...gave Him an honored name

...was obedient even to death   ...made every knee bow to Him

God responds to Jesus' humbling Himself by highly exalting Him. He gives Jesus a name so wonderful that it is above every other one.

What does this mean practically? That at the name of Jesus every knee would bow. Just for the record, "every" means *every* one, *all* of them, *none* are excluded. Paul "speaks slowly and uses small words" to spell out exactly how comprehensive this knee-bowing is. It entails the three different realms of existence the audience would have known: the human, earthly inhabitants; the heavenly, divine inhabitants; and the inhabitants of the underworld. This elaboration makes clear that Paul is talking about far more than just the human race. All creation will bow before Him one day—not just in His presence, but at the mention of His name! Imagine a name commanding that much honor and respect!

Which knees? "Every" knee is already comprehensive, but Paul goes to extra lengths to ensure that we don't just think he is referring to humanity. Every part of creation will pay homage to Jesus, bowing at His name.

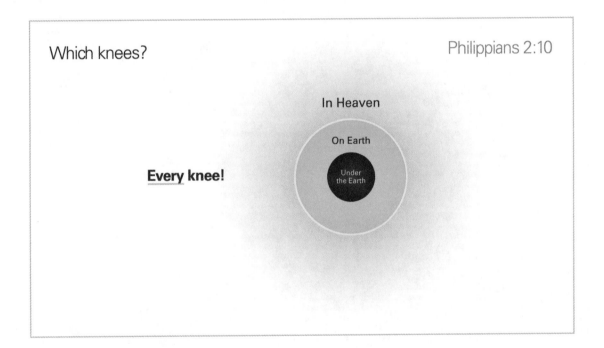

Which knees?   Philippians 2:10

In Heaven

On Earth

Under the Earth

Every knee!

So what does the humiliation and exaltation of Jesus have to do with us? Is Paul just teaching theology here? Recall from the beginning of this section that Paul cites Jesus' example as a model for us to follow. Seeing how things turned out for Him provides incentive to us as we rise to the challenge of being like-minded. If two people are butting heads, something has to give. Recall the opening verses of the chapter: Is there *any* encouragement? Is there *any* consolation or fellowship? It's so hard to place others' interests before our own because of our sinful nature. The example of Jesus not only challenges us, it casts a vision for the payoff of humbly submitting ourselves to God. We see the same relationship between humility and exaltation outlined in Jas 4:10 and 1 Pet 5:6. The path to exaltation is humility— serving others. Paul fully understands this, driving it home using Jesus' experience as the ultimate example.

In terms of Paul's flow of thought in this chapter, his big idea of being like-minded is still front and center. The example of Jesus' humiliation and exaltation in the present context is focused on motivating the Philippians to heed his call to be like-minded. Paul picks up the call for obedience in the very next section.

Philippians 2:12–18

The word connecting 2:12 to what precedes ("so then" [NET]; "therefore" [ESV]) signals Paul's return to his main line of thought: following the example of Jesus' humiliation and exaltation. Recall from 1:27 Paul's expectation that the Philippians would walk in a manner worthy of the gospel. In this present section, he once again lets the Philippians know that he expects them to obey what he has commanded. The kind of activity that he has described as like-mindedness and walking in a worthy manner is expounded upon in 2:12.

Paul sets up what he is about to say by placing it in a specific context: their track record of obedience. He once again describes it using a contrasting pair of settings. Obeying in his presence might be expected, but the Philippians have gone above and beyond this. What do you do when no one's looking over your shoulder to make sure you comply? This is essentially the position the Philippians are in because of Paul's imprisonment; even in his *absence* they obey! The reports from Epaphroditus and others would have enabled him to know how things were going. Paul is affirming their consistent obedience as the setting for his next big idea.

First Big Idea   Philippians 2:12

JUST AS YOU
ALWAYS OBEYED…
− in His presence
+ in His absence

work out
your salvation
**with fear &
trembling**

First Big Idea: This verse summarizes the various calls to action that Paul has given the Philippians: to walk in a manner worthy of the gospel (1:27), to be like-minded (2:2), and to consider others more important (2:3). Verse 12 focuses on the manner in which these actions should be implemented: with fear and trembling. Working out salvation here is referring to the practical matters of following the Lord and allowing Him to work through you. This is stressed in the very next verse, which answers why we should do this with fear and trembling: because God is the one working in us, not we ourselves (see Eph 2:10).

The working out of our salvation is not talking about matters of eternal security. Instead, the focus is on the practical matters of how we ought to live out the gospel in our daily lives. It should not be done out of arrogant confidence in our abilities, but in reverent humility. Humility is needed because it isn't *we* who are at work. Instead, it is *God* working through us to accomplish His purposes. The exhortation to fear and trembling is another safeguard for us, just like rejoicing in the Lord (see 2:1). The more self-confident we are in our conduct, the less dependent we will be on God, and the less likely we are to allow Him to work through us (see John 15:1–6).

So what exactly does "fear and trembling" really mean? Does it mean outright fear or just simple respect? When we bought our first house, there were some issues with the electrical panels that needed to be fixed before our loan would be approved. Being sort of a handy person and wanting to save some money, I decided to do the work myself. It involved installing a new circuit breaker box. The day of the project, the power company came to disconnect the power and said they would come back at 4:00 PM to hook it back up. The linemen explained to me the consequences of touching the 220 volt cables, wished me well, and then drove off. The cold sweat and knot in my stomach demonstrated my fear. It was not a debilitating fear, but one that drove me to pay the utmost attention to what I was doing—to make sure I did exactly what was expected of me. The fear was grounded (pun intended) in an accurate view of my limitations and what 220 volts could do to me.

There are some parallels between my wiring job and our relationship with God. Having too high a view of myself and my abilities (independent of God) is disastrous. Arrogance leads us to push the limits too much, to do things in our own strength. Conversely, having too low a view of ourselves is not helpful either, making us doubt God's love or purposes for us. We need to remember that God chose to redeem us for His good pleasure, making us His children and co-heirs with Christ! What could boost our self-esteem more than this?

When we contrast these two verses, there seems to be a tension between personal action and reliance on God:

> Philippians 4:13 (LEB): I am able to do all things by the one who strengthens me.

> John 15:5 (LEB): I am the vine; you are the branches. The one who remains in me and I in him—this one bears much fruit, for apart from me you are not able to do anything.

These verses actually argue the same point: apart from God working in us, we cannot accomplish anything of lasting value. This doesn't mean we should treat God like a power source or means of inspiration; God needs to be the one working in us. When He is, all things are indeed possible, but only because of His involvement.

When things get out of whack, how do I regain an accurate understanding of who God is and who I am? The best place to start is reading Scripture. It renews our understanding of who He is and what He has done. Although we were once God's enemies, He has delivered us out of darkness into His marvelous light (1 Pet 2:9). Here's the key to making a change: Restore a right view of God and who you are in light of Christ's work.

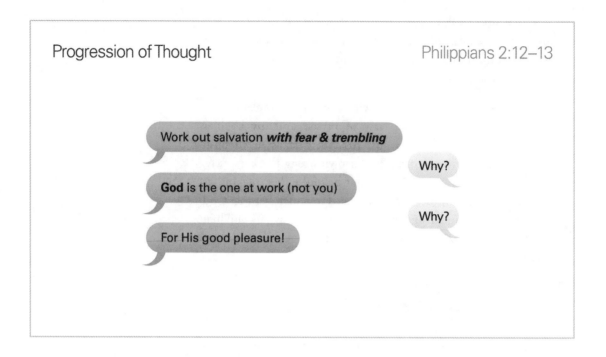

Progression of Thought — Philippians 2:12–13

- Work out salvation **with fear & trembling**
- Why?
- **God** is the one at work (not you)
- Why?
- For His good pleasure!

Progression of Thought: There is a series of supporting statements in 2:12–13 that develops in ways similar to how we might use rhetorical questions in English. The command to work out our salvation emphasizes the manner in which it should be done: with fear and trembling. The next sentence explains why we should do it in this way. It is not *us* that are the ones working it out, but God working in us. Paul tells us that God works in us not because of our righteousness or anything we have done. Instead, God works in us for His own pleasure. Thus there is no room for pride or arrogance; fear and trembling is the proper response.

The opening verses in this section form a series of supporting statements, with 2:13 supporting 2:12. It ends up developing like a question/answer dialogue in a conversation. Verse 13 says that we should work out our salvation with "fear and trembling." Why? Because *we* are not really the ones working it out; it is *God* working in us. *He* is the one at work, not us.

Why is He doing this work in us? It's not for our sake, even though we benefit immensely from His work. Taking such a view distorts both our view of God and of ourselves. Instead, He does this work for *His* good pleasure, not ours. Maintaining a proper view of God ensures that we keep a proper view of ourselves as well. When one gets distorted, the other is bound to be affected.

Paul introduces the next big idea of the section in 2:14 with the command to do all things without grumbling or complaining. This command is closely connected to the themes of 1:29–30. Paul discloses that he is not the only one who is destined to suffer for Christ; the Philippians will suffer as well—in the same manner that Paul has suffered. The call not to grumble and complain in 2:14 applies to all kinds of suffering: opposition and the daily grind of ministry. God never promised it would be easy, but He has promised to work through us to accomplish His purposes. Seeing suffering as ordained by God prevents us from wrongly assigning it to something else.

Second Big Idea

Philippians 2:14

Everything!

Do ~~most things~~ without grumbling and complaining.

Consistently living out this command means living out the other commands covered in this chapter. We must have the same humble attitude as Christ—not railing against God for disrespecting our own rights. As we maintain a Christ-like attitude—considering others better than ourselves—we're in a far better position to obey.

Some things are easier to do without complaint than others. Paul is not selective here in his command. He does not allow us to pick and choose what we'll do with a happy heart. When the suffering that Paul tells us to expect comes along, we shouldn't play the victim, decrying the lack of fairness. If God sets something before us, we're expected to do it without talking back or drawing attention to the downsides. Why give such a command? There is no greater joy-robber than grumbling and complaining. Remember the Israelites in the wilderness and all their grumbling? It coincided with stubborn rejection of God's provision for them. Rejoicing and working without grumble or complaint are inextricably related. Both stem from the attitude of the heart. The more we choose to rejoice in the Lord and be thankful for His provision, the less we'll struggle with a bad

Second Big Idea: Paul takes what could have been a bland statement and makes it comprehensive. Commanding us not to grumble or complain would have been sufficient. If it involved grumbling or complaining, we should not be doing it, right? Paul adds emphasis to "everything," which is already implied by the command not to grumble. The command to do "everything" without grumbling or complaining raises the standard—the comprehensive nature of the command is explicit instead of implicit.

attitude. One is a natural consequence of the other; this is how God has ordained things to work.

At this point, it seems like Paul has shifted gears away from the topic of advancing the gospel (Phil 1), but 2:15–16 make it clear that this is not the case. Why should we rejoice in all things instead of grumbling and complaining? What should be our motivation for obeying? What is at stake? The answer might surprise you. In Paul's mind, these calls to specific behavior are about shining God's light in a dark and dying world. Not only will obedience draw us closer to God and help us experience His blessing, it also accomplishes God's larger purpose.

Just as avoidance of grumbling and complaining is a natural consequence of thankfulness and rejoicing, we can shine for Christ by being blameless and innocent. Our goal isn't to put down the crooked and perverse generation with our self-righteousness. Instead, Paul says the goal is to advance the gospel—the theme with which he opened the book. Equipping and challenging others to be more obedient to Christ is one way Paul effectively advances the gospel while in prison. By multiplying himself in others, the gospel is able to advance exponentially.

Verse 16 closes by raising (and essentially dismissing) the possibility that Paul's ministry efforts have been in vain. In 2:17, he likens his labor to being poured out as a drink offering—which is a positive thing. The word "even" found in most translations creates a thematic connection with 2:16: His current situation might call into question whether his effort was really worth it. Just like his response in 1:18, he responds to this question with rejoicing. In 2:18, he calls the Philippians to respond like him. In doing this, Paul once again redefines what success looks like for him (compare 1:21). Success does not require his comfort or even his continued existence. Success does not require the Philippians' comfort or freedom from pain or hardship. In Paul's view, success comes by allowing God to accomplish His purposes through our lives. Paul sees that in the midst of hardship, this will come about—that's why it's cause for rejoicing for him and the Philippians.

Philippians 2:19–24

In this section, Paul shifts gears from personal matters to personnel matters, concerning Timothy and Epaphroditus. Although it might seem at this point that we're reading someone else's private correspondence, Paul accomplishes much more here than updating the Philippians on his plans. Paul begins by praising Timothy for the qualities that have made him an invaluable member of his team. But more than just giving Timothy a well-deserved pat on the back, Paul accomplishes something in addition: holding up Timothy as a model for other believers.

Think about what it would be like to have a godly leader affirm you like Paul does Timothy. How would it make you feel? How might it boost your motivation to persevere in the midst of difficult circumstances? I often wonder what Paul was like. I do not imagine him offering praise lightly or coddling those who wavered in their commitment. Remember what happened to Barnabas' nephew John Mark in Acts 15:36–41. Since his departure from ministry was taken by Paul as abandonment, he was unwilling to take him on another missionary journey. I imagine Paul was a no-nonsense guy. Think about how significant it would be to hear this kind of affirmation from someone who probably didn't regularly praise others.

It seems that we often forget that the praise wasn't only for Timothy's benefit. When we hear a leader publicly praised, we are challenged to be like them. It raises the bar for all leaders from status quo to a higher standard.

WANTED

WORKERS WHO ARE:

- Like-minded
- Genuinely Concerned for the Church
- Seeking after Christ's Interest Before Their Own
- Posessing Proven Character

First Big Idea: Paul was not afraid to openly praise individuals with whom he worked in ministry and to hold them up as examples for others to follow. Timothy is no exception. Such recognition is rare these days, perhaps because we're concerned about puffing up the ego of the one being praised. Although the qualities that Paul highlights are found in Timothy, they could be found in almost anyone who diligently devotes themselves to ministry. So while the praise may serve to build up Timothy, it also promotes Timothy as a role model. The qualities that are praised are like a job description for others to aspire toward. Paul presents himself as an example to follow in 3:1. His affirmation of Timothy in 2:19–22 has a similar function.

With each characteristic that Paul affirms in Timothy, we are challenged to reconsider how *we* are doing in that area. Would Paul say the same thing about *us*? If not, what would it take to be more like Timothy? What was it that he did that made the difference? What would that look like in my ministry setting?

Fear of puffing up someone's ego is too often used as an excuse for avoiding praise, whether public or private. Too often I've done this very thing or ignored an opportunity to praise someone in the name of being task-oriented or realistic. Each time I do, I disregard the clear command of 1 Thessalonians 5:11 to encourage one another and build each other up. Taking the view that "I said I valued you in the beginning, and if anything changes I'll let you know" cannot be supported by Scripture. We should not recklessly praise or promote others; 1 Timothy 3:6 provides a warning to make sure a leader's maturity matches their ministry responsibility. Neglecting this just sets them up for a fall.

There is no right answer about exactly how much praise is too much. It is a matter of balance determined by the needs and context. But as we seek this balance, we must take care that the pendulum does not swing too far one way or the other. In my experience, we need to be doing a whole lot more praising and building up to move the pendulum to where it should be.

So what were the traits for which Paul praises Timothy? There are two primary things. The first is introduced as like-mindedness with Paul (2:20), what we might also call being a soul mate. This doesn't imply that there was never disagreement but more likely that their core values and priorities meshed well together, that they were on the same page when it came to ministry. What is more, he was genuinely concerned for the Philippians' welfare

Why would this be such a big deal to Paul? In 2:21 he supports his previous statement by noting that most people seek their own interests rather than the interests of Jesus Christ, the latter of which characterized Timothy. He was not like all the rest, looking out for himself first.

Sidebar on Timothy: Once again Paul makes a series of statements beginning with "for," where each supports the one before, but does not advance the big idea. Instead, these statements serve to strengthen or flesh out some aspect of what precedes. In English, we would much more naturally use rhetorical "Why?" questions to let people know that what follows answers the question posed. The "therefore" in 2:23 signals the return to the specific idea of sending Timothy and the end of the series of support statements. Another series of support statements begins in 2:25.

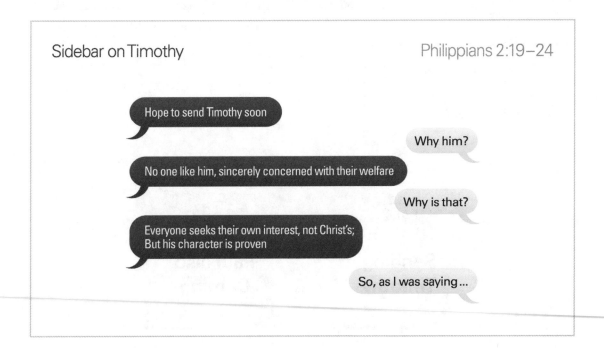

Sidebar on Timothy   Philippians 2:19–24

Hope to send Timothy soon

Why him?

No one like him, sincerely concerned with their welfare

Why is that?

Everyone seeks their own interest, not Christ's;
But his character is proven

So, as I was saying...

Paul also mentions Timothy's proven character, spelling out more precisely what that looks like at the end of 2:22. How was his character proven? By Timothy's devoted service to Paul that could accurately be likened to a son's devotion to his father, serving faithfully by his side. For these reasons, Timothy is Paul's go-to guy when it comes to sending someone to the Philippians to minister on his behalf because of his imprisonment. It is for these same reasons that Timothy can also he held up as a model leader whom others could appropriately look up to and model themselves after.

There's one more thing to note in this section on Timothy. Paul opens it by saying he intends to send him to them soon, then goes off on a supporting sidebar about why. When he returns to the issue of sending him, he adds a new twist, highlighting it by dropping a "first shoe" that anticipates a second one dropping soon. Instead of just affirming his earlier statement, he uses words with the Greek equivalent of "Although I am hoping to send him soon … ." Why? It creates anticipation from the very beginning that something more is coming and is probably more important. It would be just like me saying, "While I liked your introduction … ." You would know as soon as you hear "while" that something more was coming, that this comment was not the last one on the matter. The same holds true for Paul.

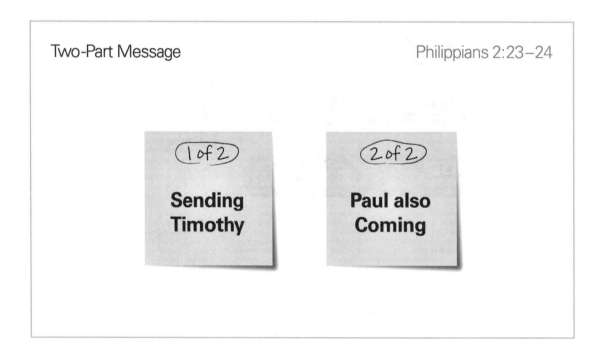

Two-Part Message   Philippians 2:23–24

(1 of 2)   (2 of 2)

Sending Timothy   **Paul also Coming**

Using this "first shoe dropping" strategy creates anticipation for the thing that follows. What's that thing? Paul's expectation that Timothy won't be the *only* one visiting them soon (using "only" here is another way of accomplishing the same task in English, by the way). *Paul also* intends to come (emphasized in Greek), and not just to send Timothy as an emissary. His goal in telling them about Timothy's arrival was to give them confidence that he would continue to support their ministry. Imagine the thrill at hearing about his intention to visit. Paul's use of this special device gives us some insight into his relationship with the Philippian believers. He cared enough not just to mention his desire to visit, but to attract extra attention to it.

From the outset of the book, Paul's focus has been on the advance of the gospel. Although his focus has shifted from changing the Philippians' perspective about his situation to the matter of sending Timothy, there is still a focus on the gospel. How? By holding up this man as a role model of godly leadership for others to imitate and aspire to be like. The list of qualities that Paul praises could just as easily have been a job description for the kind of worker Paul wanted. His praise of Timothy not only affirmed him in the eyes of the church, it undoubtedly edified him personally to hear it. We cannot underestimate the power of well-placed affirmation. Although we must guard against puffing up someone's ego, we cannot use this as an excuse to ignore commands in Scripture like Rom 12:10 and 1 Thess 5:11 to build one another up.

Philippians 2:25–30

Understanding the situation with Epaphroditus is like listening to half of a phone conversation in that we only know the details that Paul has included in the letter. Apparently the Philippians had sent Epaphroditus to minister to Paul in prison on behalf of their church, most likely with a gift of some kind. Somewhere along the way, Epaphroditus got sick enough that he nearly died. Word spread pretty slowly in those days, determined largely by being able to send word via someone else from one place to another. Apparently the illness lasted long enough for them to not only hear he was sick, but also for word to come back that they were concerned for him and his mission.

Paul unpacks things a little differently than what we're used to in English. He starts at the conclusion and works back to the beginning using a series of "for" statements. Why would Paul do this? Epaphroditus getting sick and being sent home was a lot bigger deal than you might think—I'll discuss this more below.

Note that Paul doesn't just announce that Epaphroditus is being sent home, but that it is "necessary" for him to go. This isn't because of Epaphroditus' sickness, but because of the distress his sickness is causing. The Philippians had heard he was sick—really sick. Paul orders it this way so that we know that Epaphroditus is not being sent back because of his sickness or seemingly failed mission. He's being sent back to alleviate the angst of the Philippian congregation. Epaphroditus being welcomed back into the Philippian church is a relief for him and Paul. The last part of 2:27 makes it sound as though Paul didn't want the liability of having him potentially die on his watch.

Sidebar on Epaphroditus

Philippians 2:25–30

Necessary to send Epaphroditus

Why?

He was longing for them and distressed

Why?

They heard he was sick

Seriously?

Seriously, nearly died. Instead, God had mercy on him (and me!)

So as I was saying ...

Eagerly sending him

Why?

So they'd rejoice and Paul would relax

How should they respond?

Welcome with all joy, hold such ones in high regard

Sidebar on Epaphroditus: As in 2:19–24, this section has an extended series of supporting statements introduced by "for." Each one serves to strengthen some aspect of what precedes, but often it's a sidebar when it comes to advancing the main idea. All of this information explains the circumstances behind Epaphroditus' premature return home. More importantly, these supporting statements direct the Philippians in how they ought to process the situation and how to receive him back. Has he failed? Could something more have been done? Was it worth sending him in the first place? Who knows what kinds of thoughts were floating around in his home church. Paul's strategy is to demonstrate how one thing has led to the next, affirming that Epaphroditus has by no means failed, nor is he being disavowed by Paul. His return is as much for Paul's sake as that of the Philippians, and they should hold him and others like him in high regard.

All of this builds toward the situation that Epaphroditus could have faced when returning home. It raises the question of how the Philippians should receive him. According to the values of the day, Epaphroditus could have been viewed as a failure. Shame and honor played a huge role in Greek and Roman society.

Even though this value system doesn't play a big role in our culture, it is nonetheless present. Imagine having a huge gathering of family and friends over for a Thanksgiving feast. Everything is ready, all the seats are filled, and all that's left is to bring out the turkey. Now imagine that as you're carrying the turkey in, you trip over the cat, completely dump the turkey on the floor, and end up landing on top of it, pulverizing it into an inedible mess. How would you react in that situation (other than wanting to kill that cat)? Yes, there is the task of carrying the turkey that was left incomplete, but you'd likely feel something more. There would be the embarrassment of not seeing the cat and falling. There would be shame and mortification of having invited people who expected a wonderful meal, and then having nothing but potatoes and cranberry salad to offer them. Imagine how the guests would feel. Not only would they be disappointed, but they would probably be embarrassed for you. They might not even know how to respond. Do they tell a joke? Do they offer to help clean up, or would that just make matters worse?

Let's take a look at this through the lens of shame and honor. The person who dropped the turkey would definitely feel a sense of shame, but he or she would not be alone. Their spouse would feel the same as well. Is their family going to be remembered every Thanksgiving as the ones who ruined the turkey in front of their guests? Will the relatives harass them for years? What will this event do to the host's or hostess' confidence? How long would it be, if ever, until they would invite a large group over again? Okay, we may not fall on the sword or jump out of a window when we make big mistakes, but we can understand the shame it can bring. We can imagine how we would carry the dishonor with us. Now let's go back and revisit the scenario recounted in Phil 2:25–30.

Epaphroditus was specifically sent to Paul to minister to him. This would have resulted in both Epaphroditus and the Philippians receiving honor from Paul. However, things did not go as planned. Rather than Epaphroditus serving Paul, one of the people there with him ended up having to serve Epaphroditus, caring for him until he got better. Instead of being a blessing from the Philippians, Epaphroditus was a burden for Paul and the others to carry. This is the "falling on the turkey" moment. Even though the sickness may have been beyond his control, it would nonetheless have resulted in bringing dishonor to both Epaphroditus and the sending church. Imagine how they and Epaphroditus would have felt.

Shame and honor are funny things; they're in the eye of the beholder. Paul could have shamed the Philippians and Epaphroditus, but instead he demonstrates God's grace in action. He could have gone prima donna on them, complaining about the imposition Epaphroditus' sickness caused, but he doesn't. Imagine we are back at the Thanksgiving feast. You have just stood up after falling and are brushing turkey off your shirt. There is a horrendous silence as everyone is embarrassed and afraid to speak. What if the most respected hostess present—the Martha Stewart of the bunch—stood up to help and began to tell a story about how she did something far worse? The incident would not go away, but it would be positively spun.

Honor is a commodity to be given or withheld. Those in highly respected positions have the opportunity to heavily influence the outcome in such situations, just like Paul did with Epaphroditus. Because he chose to spin the situation as a positive thing instead of an imposition—to hold Epaphroditus up as a blessing instead of a burden—Paul allowed both Epaphroditus and the Philippians to save face. Paul removes whatever shame may have been felt and strengthens relationships in doing so.

Let's take a look at how Paul's language bears out this idea of shame and honor being at stake. Twice in 2:25 Paul refers to him as a "fellow." Why? Remember, the most highly respected person holds the cards. They can lift someone up or push them down. Picture someone you really look up to telling a group of people about the difference you have made in their life. Talk about a boost—not only for your own view of yourself, but for others' view of you as well!

Perspectives on Epaphroditus: Like the applauding of Timothy in 2:19–22, the discussion of Epaphroditus' ministry holds him up as a model Christian worker. Imagine how you would feel if someone like Paul praised you like this. While it might be humbling, it would also provide incentive to "keep up the good work." And for those around you, it would highlight key qualities to which to aspire. In the case of Epaphroditus, Paul's affirmation considers him from two different perspectives: that of Paul and that of the Philippians. To Paul, Epaphroditus was a fellow worker, fellow soldier, and brother. Paul's affirmation of Epaphroditus' character and service corrected any notion that he was a failure because of his sickness.

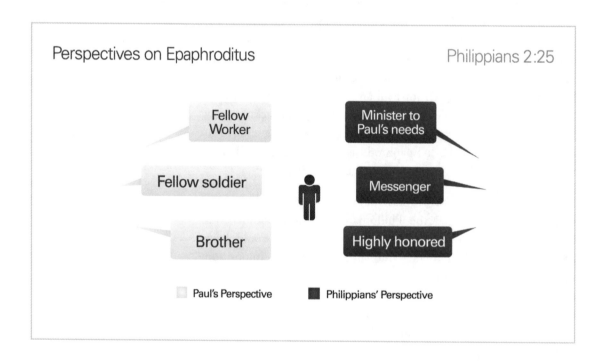

Perspectives on Epaphroditus   Philippians 2:25

Fellow Worker

Fellow soldier

Brother

Minister to Paul's needs

Messenger

Highly honored

☐ Paul's Perspective   ■ Philippians' Perspective

Paul does better than this, referring to Epaphroditus as though he were an equal. Just imagine what that would have been like! Characterizing Epaphroditus in this way would have significantly reshaped the Philippians' view of him if there was any doubt, but Paul goes on. He also tells them how *they* should view Epaphroditus and his mission.

Epaphroditus was a minister to Paul's needs, not a burden—a messenger, not a mess. Instead of needing to skulk away in shame, he is to be highly honored by them. Epaphroditus' career in ministry could quite easily have ended as a result of these events. Bad things happen that are beyond our control. Sometimes they happen as a natural consequence of something we did wrong. If you are in a respected position of leadership, you have a huge influence over the fallout and long-term harm from such a situation. How you respond sets the tone for those who look up to you; your reaction will help shape theirs.

Philippians 3

Philippians 3:1–4a

The transition into this chapter is abrupt. Paul has explained his response to imprisonment and rival preachers, as well as how the Philippians should respond. He transitions from telling them to expect the arrival of Timothy, Epaphroditus, and (hopefully) himself to instructing them and encouraging them. The instructions that follow are based more on *their* situation than on his, which is one reason his tone changes. The opening word translated "finally" is translated elsewhere as "the rest" or "others." It signals that he is moving on to other matters. It does not mean this is the last thing he has to say.

So of all the things he could begin by saying, what does Paul exhort them to do? It turns out that he beats the same drum he beat earlier: to rejoice (see 1:18; 2:17–18). Why is rejoicing so important to Paul? Does he just want us to smile and be happy for Jesus? Think about the contexts so far where Paul has either declared that he rejoices/will rejoice, or where he has exhorted the Philippians to do so. They are not situations that we would characterize as happy; these statements are found in the midst of hardship. Rejoicing is an activity we *choose* to do; it is not an emotion. If we choose to rejoice, it means we are choosing *not* to do something else. Paul here gives us a key insight into life that we cannot afford to miss.

God, in His infinite wisdom, has ordained things to work a certain way. One of those things concerns our attitude or focus in life. If we are truly rejoicing and thankful for God's provision, we cannot complain or be resentful. It doesn't work that way; this is by design. What comes out of our mouths (for better or worse) is an indicator of what is going on in our hearts (see Matt 15:18; Luke 6:43–45). What do our words say about our attitude, heart, and focus?

This mutual exclusivity is a great thing for us. If we focus our efforts on rejoicing in God and in His provision, we are at the same time guarding against things that rob us of our joy. This is why Paul is able to characterize rejoicing as a "safeguard"; he understood how God has wired us. It's like the old saying that "the best defense is a good offense." Choosing to go on the offensive by rejoicing in the midst of hardship is the *single greatest defense* from the things that make us turn away from God.

By making the choice to rejoice in the Lord in the midst of unpleasant circumstances, we will guard ourselves against fear, doubt, double-mindedness, and the discouragement that comes from opposition. All of these things are barometers for our heart attitude. As we see these things creeping in and manifesting themselves, we know that our focus is shifting away from God and onto other things. I cannot complain about something and simultaneously be thankful for it.

Rejoicing as a Safeguard:
Paul begins the chapter by *again* commanding the Philippians to rejoice. It is one of the most critical things they can do to guard their hearts against discouragement. It's not just a good idea, it is a safeguard specifically designed by God for this purpose. How does it work? If I am choosing to rejoice in the Lord whatever my circumstances or situation, it will be nearly impossible to grumble and complain about them. It is an either/or proposition. A natural consequence of truly rejoicing in the Lord about something is the inability to complain about it. You cannot grumble and rejoice about the same thing at the same time. If you're grumbling, you're not rejoicing.

Rejoicing as a Safeguard   Philippians 3:1–2

Paul begins Philippians 3 by describing rejoicing in the Lord as a safeguard because he is going to warn them about people in their lives who are seeking to rob them of their joy in 3:2. Paul references the same group of people in three different ways: dogs, evil workers, and mutilators. The next verse implies that these people are not the true circumcision; he claims "we [Paul and the Philippian believers] are." What he means by this is elaborated upon in the rest of 3:3. The true circumcision worships the Spirit of God (as opposed to something else); they boast in Christ Jesus and put no confidence in the flesh.

Philippians 3:4b–11

Boasting on the basis of the flesh is to be avoided. Yet in the very next verse, Paul is going to ignore that fact. The word that introduces 3:4 signals that what follows somehow contradicts what he's just said, not unlike adding a "but if I was *gonna* do this … ." He takes up the idea of boasting hypothetically, challenging anyone who thinks they can beat him in a comparison of flesh-based titles or awards.

Hypothetically Speaking: Paul sets the stage for one of his most significant declarations by essentially saying we should never do such a thing. Even though Christians are not to put confidence in the flesh, Paul does it anyhow to make the point that in the end, there really is nothing worth boasting about other than being found in Christ with a righteousness that comes through faith in God. The Greek in the first part of 3:4 could be paraphrased "but if I was *gonna* do it … ." He says not to do something, and then he does it in excess to make a sobering point about the incomparable worth of knowing Christ.

Hypothetically Speaking...   Philippians 3:2–3

Worship by the Spirit of God
Boast in Christ Jesus
No confidence in the flesh...

But if I was **gonna** do it...

And so begins a list of credentials that would have made any Jew of his day envious. It's like he is daring anyone to try to one-up him: "You think you've got a claim to make? We'll just see about that!"

What trophies and accolades does he have hanging on his wall, figuratively speaking? Heritage, schooling, zealous exploits—he's got it all. He was circumcised on the eighth day, just as specified in Lev 12:3—a full-blooded Israelite even though he hailed from Tarsus. And he's not just any Israelite. He's from the tribe of one of Jacob's two most-favored sons: Benjamin. As far as religious education, his reference to being a Pharisee implies adherence to a strict interpretation of the Torah according to their customs. His statement about persecuting the church makes him a bona fide Pharisee. His connection to Pharisaism was more than casual; it singularly directed his actions. His lifestyle also bore out his commitment to living a righteous life. Paul is not talking here about a works-based righteousness but a life characterized by strict obedience to the Pharisaic code; he lived it out blamelessly.

Paul's Trophy Wall: Paul boasts in the flesh by creating a figurative trophy wall of his qualifications and accomplishments. From the standpoint of first-century Judaism, he had impeccable credentials. This list of accomplishments is just a set-up; they will all soon be figuratively cast aside on the dung heap. But until that point, he makes his trophy wall sound as desirable as possible—the more envy the better.

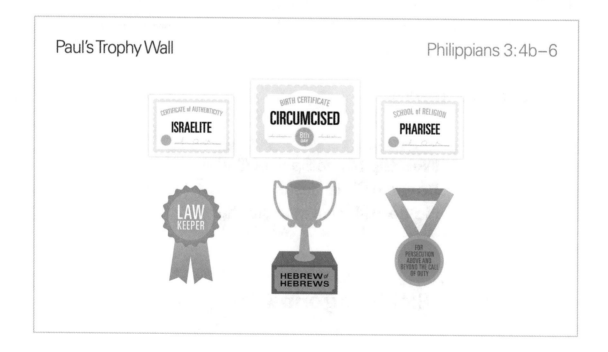

Paul's Trophy Wall   Philippians 3:4b–6

CERTIFICATE of AUTHENTICITY
ISRAELITE

BIRTH CERTIFICATE
CIRCUMCISED
8th DAY

SCHOOL of RELIGION
PHARISEE

LAW KEEPER

HEBREW of HEBREWS

FOR PERSECUTION ABOVE AND BEYOND THE CALL OF DUTY

This survey of Paul's religious credentials proves that if anyone had a right to claim a favored status and to wield religious influence over his peers, it was Paul far more than the Judaizers he references in 3:2. If the Philippians wanted to put someone on a religious pedestal, Paul is the guy who deserves it.

Now remember that he clearly stated in 3:3 that no one was to put confidence in the flesh, period. So why does he show off all of his accomplishments? He does this to illustrate just how much he is willing to give up in exchange for knowing and being identified with Christ. It's one thing to say that you would give up everything to follow Christ, and quite another to list and sign over all of your most prized assets. The latter is exactly what Paul is doing. By showing the incalculable value of all that he was willing to give up, Paul raises the value of knowing Christ. He does this in several stages.

In the first stage, he essentially says, "You want to know how committed I am to Christ, how important He is to me? You see all these things I just listed, all the things on my trophy wall? I'm willing to write off *all these things* for the sake of Christ." These are the things that would have given Paul respect, honor, and influence in his culture, yet he's willing to disavow them in exchange for knowing Christ.

What are the things that you have on your trophy wall? For me, it would be my graduate degrees, publications, how smart and wonderful my kids are, my lovely wife (the most gracious hostess you're ever going to meet), and my ability to build or fix things. All of these things in one way or another can build my ego; they're things that I can beat my chest about and say, "Hey, look at me!" What's interesting about Paul's trophies is that half of them were completely beyond his control: being an Israelite of Benjamin and an eighth-day circumcision. These were sovereignly bestowed!

Consider Trophies Loss

Philippians 3:7

Considers Trophies Loss: Paul hypes the value of his trophy wall to make giving them away seem all the more significant. He does not downplay the worth of these things; he increases the value of knowing Christ. What Paul considers most valuable, he is willing to exchange for knowing Christ. But wait, there's more.

So what exactly does Paul mean when he counts these things as loss? If I want to be like Paul, do I need to burn my degrees, stop using my building knowledge, and be ashamed of my family? No. As we look at the account of his life in Acts, we never see him pretending that he was not an influential, well-connected Jew and a Roman citizen. We regularly see him utilizing his knowledge of the Law, Pharisaism, and his Jewish heritage. He used any advantage he could to further the gospel. What he is talking about here is *where he finds his identity*. He is honing in on a million-dollar question: Where do we place our value—what parts of our life in the flesh do we boast about? The answer should be "none." These are all valuable things, but they are to be used as gifts from God for His purposes working through us.

What does this mean for me? If I'm really good at Greek, construction, or howling with my spaniel, I should not use these things to boost my ego. They should not define who I am. Think about the change in attitude that comes about when this happens. Instead of things to cling onto, all these valuable things are resources to be laid at the Lord's feet to be used for His good pleasure. In finding my identity in Christ, these other things do *not* cease to exist; they simply no longer define who I am. It's a process, not an event. Paul stresses this in 3:12–14. But it all begins by taking those things that we hold dear and no longer finding our identity in them. This is what Paul means by taking his valued trophies and counting them loss.

This sounds like an impressive sacrifice, and it is! By giving up his most treasured things, Paul makes a relationship with Christ sound valuable. But this is just the beginning! It's time for stage two. Paul raises the bar in 3:8 by saying he's willing to give up even more: *everything*! It's not just his trophies and accomplishments that he's willing to count as loss; he's willing to give it *all*! We're talking about *everything* here, not just his influence and education. He would even be willing to give his life. This is how he can say in 1:21 that "to live is Christ and to die is gain." It isn't *his* life anymore. Knowing Christ and being found in Him is worth more than anything and worth giving everything. Jim Elliot echoed this sentiment when he said, "He is no fool who gives what he cannot keep to gain that which he cannot lose." This is exactly the kind of value system that Paul describes here in Philippians 3.

Considers All Things Loss:
Here's the next stage in Paul's description of how much he values knowing Christ. It's like he's asking, "How much would you expect me to pay for all of this?" Instead of lowering the price, he increases it. Paul not only considers his trophies to be worth exchanging for knowing Christ, it's worth giving *everything*. He raises the ante. He sees the trophies and raises the stakes with *everything else*.

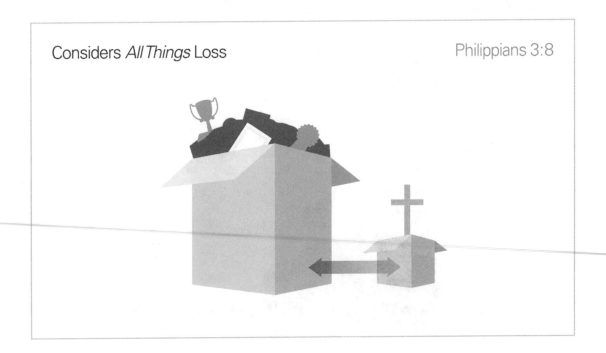

Considers *All Things* Loss   Philippians 3:8

Now for stage three. Paul ratchets things up one more notch in the last half of 3:8. This time he makes us a little uncomfortable. When we have something of value in our culture, say a house or a car, we typically insure it against loss from fire, theft, or various kinds of destruction. We do this because we want protection against loss. When Paul says that he counts all things loss, he is still treating them as valuable. He is simply making the decision not to hang onto these valuable things, but to exchange them for Christ. In this last stage, all this changes.

Paul is about to talk about the things we deposit in toilets. Most of us today have toilets in our homes, workplaces, and pretty much any public place. All the toilets are connected to soil pipes that take away the things that have been deposited there. Where? Nobody really cares where, so long as it is gone. Why aren't we sad when we flush the toilet? Because we have absolutely no interest in keeping what is deposited there! We pay utility companies to take it.

Instead of Paul considering all his stuff as "valuable, but worth the trade" for knowing Christ, Paul goes one step further. Knowing Christ is so valuable to him that, in comparison, he considers his stuff to be about as desirable as feces.

Considers all things what?

What's left after putting everything on the table in exchange for knowing Christ? Maybe not what you'd expect. So far he has treated the things he's willing to trade for knowing Christ as though they were something worth keeping. By any human standard, they are priceless! So how can he raise the stakes further? By saying that, in his view, these priceless things aren't worth crap, literally. That's the analogy he uses. All the things that we hold dear should be considered just as valuable as a bag of feces. In comparison to the value of knowing Christ, Paul's most prized possessions aren't worth squat.

Considers all things *what*?   Philippians 3:9

Feces are not something we cling to or lament the loss of. The same was true back in the first century, which is exactly why Paul uses the term for feces or dung. He devalues the things that the world says we should treasure. He shifts from saying it is worth giving up everything to saying he considers everything but Christ valueless. It isn't even worth insuring or filing a claim for. It's no longer a "loss," it's "good riddance!" Instead of finding his identity in these things, he casts them all on the dung heap. If that's really what all our stuff is worth compared to knowing Christ, who wouldn't want to make this exchange?

Paul masterfully works his way through this illustration one stage at a time to move *us* through the process with him. As he lists his most prized possessions, it makes us wonder about what it would look like for us. He isn't so much devaluing them as he is increasing the value of knowing Christ. In the final analysis, they are less than worthless compared to the surpassing greatness of knowing Christ. We would have to be stupid not to follow his lead.

In 3:9–10, Paul elaborates on exactly what is involved in the exchange. He states both what life in Christ is and what it is not. It is *not* a righteousness of his own, the kind that comes from the Law. This is the kind of righteousness from a life well-lived that he alluded to at the end of 3:6. The added descriptors—"*my* righteousness *from the Law*"—sets the stage for a contrastive parallel with the kind of righteousness he actually receives. Instead, Paul will be found in Christ with a righteousness "through faith in Christ," the kind *from God* instead of from himself.

We can know the power of Christ's resurrection—His conquering of sin and death. No longer must we live as slaves to our sinful nature and in fear of death and judgment. In Christ, we may experience freedom and deliverance from the power of sin. We can have confidence in Christ's work on the cross. We will receive an inheritance in God's kingdom because of it.

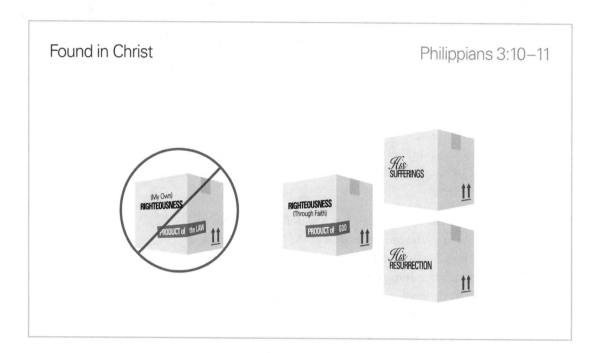

Found in Christ

Philippians 3:10–11

Found in Christ: Paul goes to great lengths to draw the contrast between the human-based righteousness that some strive for and the kind that originates from God on the basis of faith. God's righteousness comes with some unexpected peripherals: knowing the power of his resurrection and the fellowship of his sufferings. Paul makes clear that the kind of relationship with God that he has in mind is not centered on our personal comfort but on being conformed to the image of Christ.

Another thing Paul looks for is fellowship in Christ's sufferings. Identifying ourselves with Christ means embracing everything about Him, including setting aside our rights and entitlements (described in 2:5–11). It entails being humble and obedient like Jesus—obedience even to death. This is the ultimate commitment. We cannot take only the good, happy aspects of Jesus' life.

What is the goal of this kind of total identification with Christ? What's Paul's objective? What he describes in 3:11 is a hope, not something he is owed. This is not to say that he had no confidence that it would come about, only that it is not phrased as something which God owes him. If the righteousness really was of his own doing, then one might view it as an obligation on God's part (see Rom 4:4–5). Paul makes his sacrifices out of love for Christ, not as a means of earning salvation. The latter is a hope; the former is the motivation.

Philippians 3:12–14

Lest we think of Paul as some super-apostle who has a picture-perfect relationship with Christ, he shatters any such notions by declaring that he has not arrived. The declaration is made using two negative statements about what has *not yet* happened before moving on to the positive statement. The two negatives in the first part of 3:12 create suspense by delaying the introduction of the positive. He states that he has not already received [fill in the blank], or already been made perfect—raising the question of what [fill in the blank] is since it is left unstated. This is perfectly acceptable ambiguity in Greek, but it leaves some question about exactly what he has in mind.

The key thing that Paul wanted to receive, the thing on which all else hinged, was a righteousness through faith in Christ (see 3:9). He adds that this righteousness is from God on the basis of faith, the result being that he may attain resurrection from the dead (3:11). The parallel statement in 3:12 helps define what he receives. He is being made perfect and is receiving a perfect righteousness from God. The righteousness has nothing to do with his works or merit but with God's gift—given on the basis of faith. This righteousness is what qualifies him to partake in the resurrection. By leaving the [fill in the blank] unstated, Paul is referring to the concepts discussed in 3:8–11, the key one being God-given, faith-based righteousness. Remember, these statements reflect what he has *not yet* received—consistent with the hope of all things being fulfilled at Christ's return (see 3:20–21; see also Rom 3:23; Heb 9:28). Although we have been pledged these things on the basis of faith, there is nonetheless a "not yet" element as we await the fulfillment of all things. Paul essentially repeats

Paul's Big Idea: Paul draws attention to the positive thing he does (in contrast to the two negative counterpoints of 3:12). He uses the Greek equivalent of saying, "Hey, guess what!" or "Get this!" In both cases, there is a reference ahead to some concept that is yet to be introduced. Doing this does two things: It adds an extra reference to the idea, and it delays the introduction of it with the extra reference.

the same statements about *not yet arriving* at the begining of 3:13, building further toward a climactic statement in 3:13–14.

As Paul shifts from what he is *not* doing to what he *does* do, he uses a special device to draw attention to his statement. By making reference to "this" in "This one thing I do," he makes us wonder what "this" stands for. It's like he is saying, "Hey, get *this*!" in English. In both cases, attention is drawn to the following statement that defines "this." What does it refer to in 3:13–14? Three things in one complex statement.

Paul's Big Idea   Philippians 3:13–14

But **this** one thing I do:

I PRESS ON ...

The first two things serve as background for the one big thing, finally disclosed in 3:14. The two background circumstances are intentionally linked to one another using a Greek marker that is usually left untranslated. It builds the same kind of connection as using "Not only … but also …" to link things in English. Even before the original audience finished hearing about the first thing, they would have known that a second closely connected thing was coming. It's like getting a multiple-package order where each box is labeled "Item 1 of 2; Item 2 of 2." Shippers do this so that you will expect more than one thing, even if only one arrives. The same is true for using devices like this in Greek or English. It is the proverbial first shoe dropping, creating the expectation that a second one is coming.

What are the two things? The first involves forgetting what lies behind us. Dwelling on the past can be a huge hindrance to making progress on something, acting like a ball and chain holding you back. It might be dwelling on things that you regret doing or neglected to do. Think about Paul's life, how he zealously persecuted the early church. Imagine what would have happened if he had dwelt on that too much. Nothing he could have done would have been able to make it go away. We all have things that we regret. They can discourage us from believing that God can do positive things through us. Sometimes Satan is the one bringing such charges against us. For him, the next best thing to turning someone away from a close walk with Christ is to make them ineffective. But James 1:13–14 reminds us that it doesn't take divine interference to be tempted; we can do a pretty good job ourselves. Although there are indeed natural consequences for bad decisions, we need to learn our lessons and keep moving forward.

Thing One, Thing Two: Paul introduces his big idea in a specific context, set up at the end of 3:13. He does so in two parts. The first part involves letting go of the past. The way this is phrased in Greek, the original audience would have expected some related element was coming before they even finished reading or hearing the first one. It's the same kind of strategy that shippers use when they label boxes: "Box 1 of 2." If they didn't do this, we would only expect one box. The Greek word is usually left untranslated since there is no good English counterpart. Paul uses the word so that the Philippians would expect that more was coming, even before they hear about letting go of the past.

Thing One, Thing Two   Philippians 3:13–14

(1 of 2)   (2 of 2)

Forgetting the past   **Straining forward**

I PRESS ON ...

What about the alternative, dwelling on *good* things that happened in the past? What could possibly be wrong with that? Plenty! We have long struggled with relying on past achievements. The expression about "resting on your laurels" refers to the days when ancient athletes received laurel wreaths as the prize for winning a race or competition. The implication is that if you're resting on past achievements, you aren't preparing for future ones. Paul had a number of amazing things happen in his life, any one of which could have resulted in him resting on his laurels.

So what does this mean practically? Does this mean that we ignore the past completely? No! If mistakes have been made, then learn from them. Make it right if possible. Do not allow it to make you think that God could never use you again. Let go and move forward. The same holds true for positive accomplishments. Savor the moment, but then move on. Living in the past can be a huge roadblock to moving forward.

We need to also *strain toward* what lies ahead. What might prevent us from doing this? Dwelling on the past is one thing. But fear of failure, apathy, or burnout can have a similar effect. I discussed a related issue in 2:12 regarding the need to have both a right view of God and a right view of ourselves. If we really understand who we are in Christ, then fear or regret shouldn't have power over us. Having a right view of ourselves helps us avoid making God smaller than He is. Paul wants us to let go of the past and strain forward.

What does Paul strain forward *toward*? It's finally disclosed in 3:14: pressing on toward the goal, the thing to which God has called him. We have all kinds of idioms in English that capture this idea:

- Keep the main thing the main thing.

- Keep your eye on the ball.

- Keep on keeping on.

Paul has already mentioned this idea in 3:12, using the same Greek words for "pressing on." He paints a great picture of the goal, the thing for which God grabbed him in the first place. God had a purpose for Paul, and he declares here that his mission in life is to pursue that purpose no matter what. Past successes and failures will not stand in the way, nor will present circumstances. Paul's seeks the prize of the upward calling, and nothing is going to distract him from pursuing it.

Philippians 3:15–21

This next section essentially answers the "So what?" question. It tells us how we ought to live in light of the upward call of God. It builds on Paul's main idea of pressing on (3:12). Recall that Paul stresses twice that he has not arrived or been made perfect, affirming that he is still very much in process. In light of Paul's standing in the community, this may have taken some of the Philippians by surprise. Based on how he begins this section however, it seems that not everyone sees themselves in process.

He addresses a hypothetical group: "as many as are perfect" (3:15). The reference to "us" in many of the translations comes from the form of the verb that Paul uses here. The idea is to call all those who think they have arrived and give them instruction. In doing so, Paul uses a much softer form of address compared to the commands he uses throughout the book. Instead of saying "Do this!" he uses the Greek equivalent of "Let's do this." Paul mitigates the directness of the instruction by including himself in the audience; he's telling himself to do the same thing.

On The Harshness Scale

Harsh
THINK
THIS WAY!

YOU SHOULD
THINK THIS WAY

LET'S THINK
THIS WAY
Gentle

On the Harshness Scale: In most of Paul's letters he is very direct and to the point. If he wants you to do something, he commands you: "Do this!" This tone stands in contrast with the letters of John and Hebrews, where the writers use a gentler, less direct "Let's do this." The inclusion of the speaker in the exhortation softens the message— it's not just the audience being confronted. This changes what could have been a harsh command into a gentler exhortation. Paul uses this approach only *twice* in Philippians (3:15 and 16). The change in tone coincides with the lead-up to addressing the conflict between Euodia and Syntyche in 4:2.

Using the less direct "Let's" is more characteristic of John's letters or Hebrews, where the instruction takes the form more of exhortation rather than direct commands. Not so in Paul's writings; he is characterized more by taking the bull by the horns, using imperatives. The difference here is that he addresses the instruction to "us" instead of just "you." It is the only part of the book that he does so.

So why would Paul be more gentle about how he addresses this? It has to do with a sensitive issue at the beginning of Philippians 4 that involves a call to unity and like-mindedness. He prepares to address it by calling everyone—including those who think they have already arrived—to think like him, to be focused on the upward call. If someone should disagree, he says "this too" God will reveal. The implication of saying "this too" is that Paul's focus on the upward calling is from *God*, not himself. Since God has revealed *this*, the idea is that God will also reveal what to do in the case of disagreement. *He'll* be the one to show them the way forward. Paul is thinking of disagreements like the one between Euodia and Syntyche mentioned in 4:2. The advice that he gives to those who think they have arrived or have already been made perfect is similar to what we see in 4:2: Be like-minded!

This conflict between Euodia and Syntyche is significant and long-running enough for Paul to have heard about it in prison. As we'll see in the next section, Paul addresses the situation by affirming the women after calling attention to the conflict. Instead of assigning blame or taking a side, he addresses the conflict in the context of calling the believers to a higher standard of Christian practice. He doesn't solve the problem for them, but instead provides the *rules of engagement*. Paul is much less direct about addressing this problem than he is the problems in Galatians or Corinthians. He begins laying the groundwork for chapter 4 by softening his tone from "Do this!" to "Let's do this."

Verse 16 provides a caveat to 15. As we are resolving disagreements—and looking to God to reveal the proper course of action—we need to hold onto God's standard. There is no room for backsliding. The maturity we have attained becomes the new minimum standard for our behavior. Here too Paul's address uses "us" instead of "you," continuing the softer tone. Since this is Paul's personal practice, he is able to exhort us in 3:17 to become "imitators of him" (emphasized in Greek). Those who follow his example—both in Philippi and those ministering to him in prison—serve as role models.

Why is Paul concerned that they have proper role models? He states in 3:18 that many live as *enemies* of the cross instead of as *role models* of it. The way he phrases it in Greek delays the disclosure of exactly who the "many" are. Paul mentions that he has spoken about them many times and even now is doing so while weeping. He takes a detour that ramps up the emotional potency of what he is telling us, while at the same time preventing us from figuring out who the "many" are.

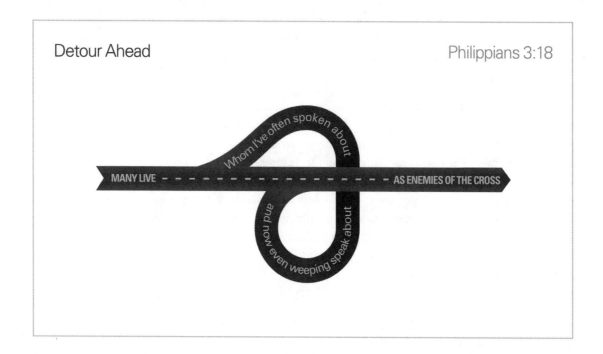

Detour Ahead   Philippians 3:18

MANY LIVE - - - - - - - - - - - - - - - - - AS ENEMIES OF THE CROSS

Whom I've often spoken about

and now even weeping speak about

Detour Ahead: Much of the focus of this section is on a group Paul refers to as "enemies of the cross." Paul draws more attention to them by delaying the disclosure of who the "many" are. He creates this delay by making two impassioned statements about the steps he has taken to warn the Philippians about such people. He's mentioned them in the past, and now weeping, he raises the issue again. This not only heightens the emotion of his plea, it also delays the disclosure of who the "many" are: *enemies* of the cross.

Paul now goes into much more detail about what he means by "enemies." He does so by contrasting them with true believers in 3:19–21.

The contrast begins with the enemies, citing a topic and then making a comment about it. The outcome of their behavior is destruction, which stands in contrast to our heavenly citizenship (3:20). Paul made the same comparison in 1:28, contrasting salvation with destruction. Next he tackles who or what they serve. In the case of the enemies, they serve their belly—something that can never be fully satisfied. In contrast, Paul references the heavenly origins of our citizenship by saying that we await the arrival of our Savior Jesus Christ from the same place. *He* is the one we serve, not our belly. In fact, Jesus tells us that if we seek first God's kingdom and His righteousness, all the other things that we need will be added (Matt 6:33).

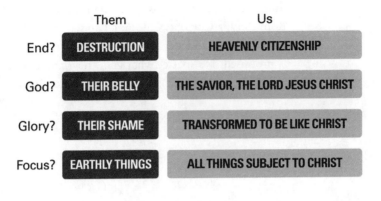

	Them	Us
End?	DESTRUCTION	HEAVENLY CITIZENSHIP
God?	THEIR BELLY	THE SAVIOR, THE LORD JESUS CHRIST
Glory?	THEIR SHAME	TRANSFORMED TO BE LIKE CHRIST
Focus?	EARTHLY THINGS	ALL THINGS SUBJECT TO CHRIST

Us vs. Them — Philippians 3:19–20

What is it that these folks take pride in? What is their glory? It's in their shame. This is not unlike those in Romans 1:32 who not only did things worthy of death, but approved of others who did the same. Here in Philippians, the enemies of the cross have their values just as mixed up. Paul contrasts this ill-placed glory with what we aspire to: having our humble bodies transformed and conformed to the glorious image of Christ. What a stark contrast! They glory in the behavior that will end in judgment and destruction, instead of salvation and glorification.

The final thing that Paul compares is focus. The enemies have their sights set on earthly things, which is to be expected of someone whose god is their stomach. The reference to heaven stands in contrast with the stuff of earth. Paul closes the reference to the believer's outlook with how things turn out. At the end of the day, Christ's glorious power enables Him to subject all things to Himself. This not only means earthly things, but everything else as well (see 2:10–11).

Us vs. Them: Paul offers contrasting portraits of the enemies of the cross in comparison with what believers may expect. In rapid succession, Paul introduces a topic and makes a comment about the enemies. After four such comments, he moves on to contrast them with what believers do or expect. The close parallels in the topics sharpen the contrast between *us* and *them*.

No matter how appealing it might look to follow these folks, the contrasting picture that Paul paints moves beyond the surface to the final outcome. Whoever they are, the Philippians want no part of what they're offering. We are repeatedly warned to watch out for those who will try to draw us away from the truth of the gospel (see Rom 16:17; 2 Cor 11:4; Gal 1:6; 1 Tim 1:3; 6:3). In the end, their ways lead to death and destruction, not the freedom and blessing that is promised. No matter what gain they may offer in the short run, following such people is a losing proposition in the end.

Philippians 4

Philippians 4:1–7

The organization of Philippians 4 hinges on the importance we place on the apparent conflict between Euodia and Syntyche mentioned in 4:2. Is it just a passing reference, or is it the central part of Paul's argument? I understand it as central. It motivates the organization and tone of Paul's message, and even the content of the message itself. We have absolutely no idea what the problem was between Euodia and Syntyche. However, based on the fact that Paul does not provide direct correction or take a side, it seems clear that the problem was not a doctrinal or moral issue. Paul elsewhere demonstrates his willingness to tackle thorny issues involving members of a church (see 1 Cor 1:12; 5:1; 2 Cor 2:1–8; Gal 1:6–10; 1 Tim 1:3–4; Philemon). If there was some specific problem that had a straightforward solution, he likely would have tackled it.

All we know about the problem is what can be gleaned from Paul's advice to the Philippians. Think back on the major themes that Paul has covered so far in the letter. Paul has not really corrected anything. Instead, he has called the Philippians to an ever higher standard of righteous living (see 1:10). He has stressed the importance of setting aside your entitlements in order to better serve those around you (see 1:27–30; 2:1–4). This is exemplified by Paul's decision to continue ministering despite his circumstances (see 1:25–26), and by citing Jesus' humiliation and obedience in the incarnation (see 2:5–11). The key components to achieving this kind of experience as a community are summarized in the calls to be like-minded (2:2), to humbly consider others to be better than yourself (2:3–4), and to choose to rejoice and be thankful even in the face of adversity (1:18; 3:1).

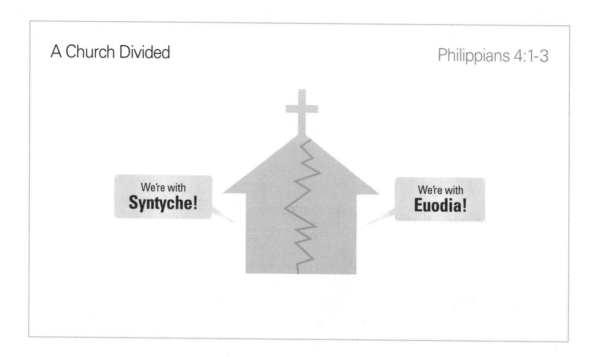

So here we have three core themes that run through the book: like-mindedness, humbly serving others, and rejoicing. All three will surface again in this section. If the conflict between Euodia and Syntyche was not a doctrinal or moral issue, it must have been an interpersonal conflict of some kind. I have found the latter to be far more divisive than the former. It usually begins as a disagreement of some kind, often over a judgment call. It is not the difference between right and wrong, but between better and best, between doing it one way versus another. Such matters are highly subjective, with "right" based on one's personal values and preferences.

If the issue is not resolved early on, it will fester. This is especially the case where efforts at reconciliation end with "agreeing to disagree." Why? Because each side leaves thinking that *they* are right, without either being willing to back down. What may have started as a small disagreement can lay the foundation for something far larger. People begin to align with one side or the other. Each is looking for a slip-up or failure of the other person that might lead to vindication: "See, she blew this opportunity just like I said she did before! It's the same cycle repeating itself." If you have been in the church for any length

A Church Divided: We have no idea what the nature of the problem was between Euodia and Syntyche. Since Paul does not take a side like he does with conflicts in other letters, this dispute is likely not about doctrine or practice. Whatever the problem, for Paul to have heard about it and had time to respond, it would have been festering for a while. So why address the problem? Why not just allow them to agree to disagree with one another? Because disagreement falls short of like-mindedness and putting others' interests before your own. How can you esteem someone as more important than yourself and simultaneously hold a grudge against them? You can't do both, which means we must be proactive about truly resolving conflict rather than allowing it to fester below the surface. A broken relationship is still broken even if there is civility on the surface.

of time, there is a good chance you have witnessed or experienced something like this unfold. Not only does it destroy relationships, it can completely distract believers from the God-given task at hand: living out the gospel in a way that attracts people to Christ. If there is unresolved conflict with people taking sides, how compelling an advertisement will this be for following Jesus?

Let's compare the concepts Paul harped on earlier with the general problems associated with interpersonal conflict. Why do we have arguments in the first place? James 4:1–2 tells us that it has to do with being envious—wanting what someone else has. Proverbs 13:12 warns us that hope deferred makes the heart sick. If we don't get what we desire, we are (naturally) unhappy. If unaddressed, disappointment can turn into anger or resentment. What keeps a conflict from being resolved? Wanting to prove that you are right? How about thinking your interests or needs are more important or worthy than those of your opponent? Most of our conflicts could be resolved by us considering others more important than ourselves, being like-minded, and choosing to rejoice instead of being resentful. When we are willing to set aside pride and emotions, we can boil down most conflicts to a few disagreements. If I really valued the other person's interests more than my own, how could I simultaneously promote my cause at their expense? If I'm truly thankful for them, how can I resent who they are or what they have?

This all sounds so simple when reading or discussing Philippians in isolation, but it gets personal in a hurry when you apply it during a dispute. "You just don't understand them or the situation." "I'm trying to show them they are wrong because I love them, but they just won't listen." Jesus ran into people who thought they had it all figured out yet needed correction, like the rich young ruler (Luke 18:18–25) or the Pharisees. No one can make other people change, not even Jesus. But we can provide people with an opportunity or challenge to change, like Jesus did with the rich ruler. Unfortunately, the man appears to have opted not to change. Paul uses the same approach here in Philippians 4, providing a challenge to the parties involved to make a change. He doesn't point a finger at them, but instead points to a higher standard of conduct—the type of conduct a godly, honorable person would strive for. If it was good enough for Jesus and Paul, it's probably a fitting strategy for us. Let's take a look.

Verse 1 is a hinge point: It partly concludes what precedes, but also introduces what follows. Based on the extensive use of terms of address (e.g., "my beloved", "my joy and crown"), we should see it as introducing the section. Imagine being called "beloved siblings," "my joy and crown." Paul commands them to "stand firm in the Lord." This is the same sentiment he expressed in 1:27 when he told them to walk in a manner worthy of the Lord so that he would hear that they were standing firm in one spirit. This might not have been the case in Philippi because of the conflict between Euodia and Syntyche.

Paul singles out two individuals—believed to be women—specifically exhorting each of them to think the same thing in the Lord. This is the very same phrase Paul used in 2:2 after corralling us into accepting his command with a series of "if there is any" statements. Since all of these conditions have been met, there is little choice but to accept the command that follows the "then." In Philippians 4, Paul specifically exhorts the women to do the same thing. The implication is that they were not getting along; they could not be characterized as being like-minded with one another. What might be viewed as a personal falling out between these individuals—perhaps agreeing to disagree, yet still harboring resentment—was affecting the Philippian church enough that Paul needed to address it.

Paul does two things in 4:3. First, he requests that his "true companion" step in and help resolve the issue. The second thing he does is somewhat surprising: He praises them. The two women whose dispute has so affected the church are positively characterized—not unlike what we see of Timothy and Epaphroditus at the end of Philippians 2. He commends their co-laboring with him in the gospel, adding that their names are written in the book of life!

Throughout this letter Paul has challenged the church to a higher calling—a total commitment to serving Christ and advancing the gospel. He has held up leaders—including himself—as role models. I noted that such affirmation would not only spur the congregation on, it would also raise the bar for the individual who is singled out. If Paul praised them and they did not apply what he commanded, imagine the effect it would have on their standing in the community! They would look like hypocrites, not the ones who *obey not only in his presence but much more in his absence* (1:12). By praising them as honorable ministers, he effectively backs them into a corner. He calls them to find an honorable resolution to their dispute. Holding their grudges and maintaining the battle lines would result in bringing shame on themselves and those who sided with them. While no one wants to admit fault in such cases, asserting their superiority and right to win—particularly after such pointed teaching about these matters in Paul's letter—would have led to significant loss of honor and standing in the community. Not resolving their dispute meant rejecting or manipulating Paul's message.

There comes a point in interpersonal conflicts where everyone loses, regardless of how it all started. The toll of backbiting, bitterness, and resentment leaves no one unscathed. It's like what we see during political campaigns today. Paul wisely presses for an end to these matters, not by choosing sides but by describing what a godly, honorable person would do. Even though the matter is only mentioned in 4:2–3, the rest of this chapter continues to address the problem by raising the standard for Christian conduct.

Paul does not provide a connecting word for relating 4:4 to what precedes. This could signal the beginning of a new and separate thought; however, all five of the statements that follow 4:2–3 omit a connecting word. I understand the command to rejoice as still addressing issues surrounding the dispute. How? Recall Paul's assertion from 3:1 that the command to rejoice would "safeguard" them from things that would turn them away from the Lord. The context of chapter 3 was opposition, whereas here it is division in the church.

The call in 4:5 to let your gentleness be known to all people raises the bar in a different way: If you are an honorable, mature believer, then those around you will see it in your gentleness. If your gentleness did not show, the implication would be that you are *not* mature. Do you see what Paul's doing here?

Safeguard Against Division

Philippians 4:4

REJOICING
IN THE LORD

Safeguard Against Division: Paul *again* commands the Philippians to rejoice. Rejoicing doesn't just guard their hearts against discouragement (3:1), but also against division. If I am choosing to rejoice in the Lord over my circumstances or situation, it will be nearly impossible to hold a grudge against those with whom I am involved. It is an either/or proposition. A natural consequence of truly rejoicing in the Lord about something is the inability to complain about the same thing. If I'm going to forgive someone, it will require me to let go of any bitterness or resentment I might harbor toward them. If you're resentful, you're not rejoicing.

There is no way you could continue to have a grudge and simultaneously exemplify gentleness. You really need to choose one or the other. The honorable thing to do in a shame/honor setting like Philippi would be to choose gentleness and let go of the grudge. The statement about the Lord being near provides a rationale for choosing gentleness. Since His return is nearing, we'd better live like it! Remember Paul's earlier call to forget the past and "strain forward" toward the goal (see 3:13–14). This also applies to personal conflicts.

The command in 4:6 not to be anxious but instead to offer prayers with thanksgiving is often understood to begin a chain of stand-alone exhortations. They are understood to be independent thoughts that do not directly relate to one another or the preceding context. I don't think this is the case. Understood in the context of resolving the conflict and restoring relationships, these exhortations make perfect sense. Any time the status quo is changed, there is inevitably some amount of anxiety. This is especially the case with fractured relationships. Even in contexts where people want to end the conflict, the unknowns of rebuilding rapport and trust can be scary. It is much easier to continue using past hurts to interpret someone's motives ("See, there they go again just like they always do!").

THANKSGIVING + (PRAYER+SUPPLICATIONS) − ANXIETY

=> **PEACE OF GOD**

Paul's command here not to be anxious but to make your requests known to God applies well to broken relationships. The caveat that the requests are to be offered with "thanksgiving"—the counterpart to rejoicing—rules out complaints or laments. Prayers like "God, please change them because they bother me" would not pass muster. Instead, the challenge is to thank God for the person or the situation—acknowledging that God is indeed sovereign and in control.

The most significant part of the command not to worry is the natural consequence of obeying it, outlined in 4:7. The peace that only God could bring—the kind that surpasses all understanding—does something incredible. Just like rejoicing is a safeguard, exchanging thankful supplications for anxiety also functions as a safeguard. God's peace will guard your heart and mind against anxiety creeping back in. Will we cling to the things that breed worry and anxiety, or will we thankfully offer them up to God? If we do the latter, God's peace will not only alleviate the stress and fear, it will also guard against its recurrence.

Paul's Formula: Paul's formula excludes wrong approaches to prayer. The prayers and supplications are to be offered with thanksgiving as opposed to other things like grumbling or resentment. They are also to be offered as an alternative to being anxious about the issues. What is the natural consequence of offering a prayer with thanksgiving? The peace of God which passes all understanding will do something amazing: It will guard your heart and mind! Against what? Anxiety, among other things. Will we cling onto the things that breed worry and anxiety, or will we thankfully offer them up to God? If we do the latter, God's peace will not only alleviate the stress and fear, it will also guard against its recurrence.

Philippians 4:8–9

This section functions as a conclusion to the last one, yet stands on its own. The opening Greek phrase generally translated as "finally" does not necessarily signal the end is near; the same term was used to introduce 3:1. Paul provides some important guidelines here about how we are to think and act. He has intentionally avoided a legalistic, narrow set of parameters. Nonetheless, the boundaries he sets are firm and sure. Let's take a closer look.

If Paul had said, "Think only about things that are true, honorable, and right," we would be left with a checklist to follow. It would essentially be a negative command, telling us not to think about things that did not meet the criteria. Instead, he has us conjure up a boundless set of items that fit positive criteria. His "whatever is" statement is like a fill-in-the-blank exercise. As long as it fits one of the criteria, you're good to go! Paul does not say, "Don't do this, don't do that, and don't do this other thing." Such a list would quickly become outdated, and we would be saying, "That doesn't apply to me today." By keeping his list general, Paul makes his message timeless. Something that is true and pure could be found in any culture or time period. Our imagination is the only limitation—other than the standards he sets.

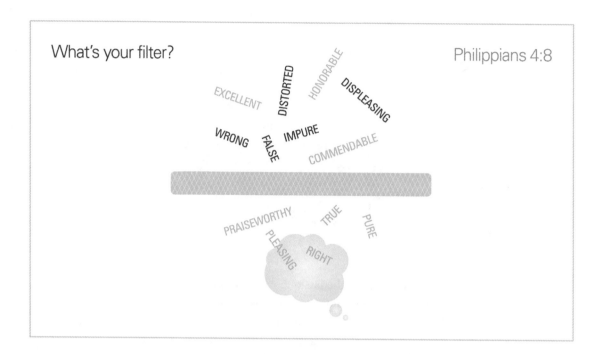

What's your filter?   Philippians 4:8

The eight criteria that Paul provides should serve as a grid for the kinds of things we ought to think about. Elsewhere he frames things from the opposite perspective, such as saying, "Let no rotten word proceed from your mouth" (Eph 4:29); even this is fairly generic, though. The list in 4:8 provides specific boundaries for determining acceptability, yet is boundless in terms of its potential for application.

The other verse in this section uses the same kind of strategy: You think of a series of things before you are told what to think about them. The focus is on behavior instead of your thought life. Instead of providing a finite list of dos and don'ts, Paul provides principles that should guide our behavior. Why? Howard Hendricks captured it well: "Rules are many, principles are few. Rules change, principles never do."

Principles are not only easier to remember because of their limited number, but they are also timeless—if properly formulated. If you tried to comprehensively list what should or should not be done, you will inevitably leave out something important. Even if you could successfully list *everything*, at some point things will change. Some new thing will come along that is a game-changer, one that falls outside the bounds of your list.

Although there are advantages to principles compared to rules, there is also a downside. Principles are few and timeless because they require thoughtful application to new situations. You cannot simply consult a list; you must analyze the situation and determine which principles are in play. Chances are high that more than one could apply—there are competing principles. Once the relevant principle is determined, often times a judgment call is required. Principles do not have right and wrong answers, but are more along the lines of good, better, and best. So while principles can bring freedom and flexibility, they can be frightening for those who are used to legalistic constraints. Although the New Testament has specific prohibitions we might characterize as rules, more often the truths of Scripture are framed as timeless principles that must be wisely implemented.

In 4:9, Paul provided a grid for deciding what kinds of things we ought to do versus not do. He avoids a specific list by giving four guidelines: "what you have learned, received, heard about, and seen in me." If what you are thinking of doing does not fit into one of the four categories, then chances are it is not edifying. This grid can be summarized by repurposing a familiar question: What would Jesus do? In this instance it is: What did Paul do or teach us to do?

What about us? How can we know what Paul would do when we have never met the guy? We see and hear about Paul's ministry in the book of Acts and in Galatians 1:11–2:14. We learn and receive teaching from him by studying his letters, like Philippians. Paul's ministry advice for handling issues that arise in the church, his personal counsel to Timothy and Titus, his praise of people like Epaphroditus and Clement, and even his affirmation of Euodia and Syntyche all help us to discern his values and decision-making processes. Looking to what Paul would do inevitably directs us back to Jesus—the author and perfector of our faith (see 1 Cor 11:1). The gospels hold more direction in matters of life and practice than we could discover in several lifetimes. Jesus is another strong proponent of principles over rules. Many of His debates with the religious leaders could be characterized as moving them beyond rules to the principles that underlie them (e.g., Luke 11:42).

Principles are a double-edged sword. The very thing that makes them timeless and broadly applicable also prevents them from being black and white in every situation. Their adaptability to new situations brings with it a measure of uncertainty since there is often not a single right answer. But the uncertainty and occasional gray area is not an excuse to create a legalistic system of rules. If this is what Paul or Jesus had intended, they would have done it themselves.

Philippians 4:10–20

In this final major section of the book, Paul addresses the support that he has received from the Philippians. There was a general allusion earlier to their participation/sharing in the gospel in 1:5, which may refer to their monetary and logistical support. There was also the discussion of Epaphroditus' ministry to Paul on their behalf (2:25). In this section he goes into more detail, but not before a sidebar on being content.

Giving someone a compliment for something they have done for you is a lot trickier than you might think. Here's what I mean. I like food, and I like it a lot. I'm very proactive about praising someone for giving me something great to eat, especially if it is something they prepared in their home. I do it first and foremost to be a courteous and thankful guest, but at times I have ulterior motives. Based on the fact that people like to be praised, there are two typical responses I have observed. The first is to offer me more of whatever it is I loved so much. If I were to say that the cheesecake for dessert was the best, richest thing I've ever tasted, chances are high that I might be offered some more. I would be lying if I said this thought had not run through my mind when framing a compliment. And there is yet another reason. If I have been a thankful guest who made the host feel great about their hospitality, there is a higher likelihood of being invited back again. For better or worse, this seems to be the nature of compliments and thanks: The more you offer, the greater the likelihood that whatever behavior generated it will be repeated.

This principle explains everything from reward-based motivation to the responses of Pavlov's dog to stimuli.

In this section, Paul is threading his way through the complexities of thank-yous. He wants to genuinely thank the Philippians for their generous gift to him, but without sounding like he is seeking more of the same. If he praises the gift too much, it will sound like he wants more. If he downplays it too much, he may sound ungrateful, or as if the gift was insufficient to meet his needs. So he does both.

He begins in 4:10 with the downplaying. At first glance it might seem like Paul is saying something like, "You're finally getting around to remembering me." He is not misspeaking; he is writing rhetorically. We do the same thing in conversation before we retract or disavow our statement: "Forget I said that; that's not what I meant." Remember, Paul is writing, not speaking. Such things are not "slips of the tongue," but a choice that implies some meaning lies behind it. He essentially repairs the first statement of 4:10 by saying that they were indeed thinking about him, but they just lacked an opportunity to express it.

At Long Last: Thanking someone for a big gift they've given you can be trickier than you might think. If there is too much praise, it may sound like you are seeking more of whatever it is they gave you. If you give too little thanks, they might think you didn't really like what they gave you. It can be a difficult balance at times. Paul handles this dilemma by essentially downplaying the Philippians' gift, preparing the way for him to richly heap praise upon them.

At Long Last   Philippians 4:10

~~Now at last you've revived your concern~~

You really were thinking about me but just lacked opportunity

---

The opportunity arose when the Philippians sent a gift with Epaphroditus. Recall from the discussion of 2:25–30 that there were questions about whether Epaphroditus' mission to Paul was a success or failure, based on his severe illness. Paul has already praised Epaphroditus' conduct, but has yet to address the gift he bore.

To understand this section, we need to recognize Paul's distinction between what is *desired* versus what is *required*. He begins with the *desired* side of things. The word in 4:11 rendered by most translations here as "need" stands in contrast to another Greek word in 4:16 that is also typically translated as "need." So what's going on here? The meaningful difference between the two is similar—not equivalent—to the difference between the English words "lack" or "shortage" and "need." The former terms refer to something that is generally quantifiable: there is not enough of something. You could be running low on something without necessarily having run out, whether it be flour, lumber, money, or milk. The latter term refers to something that is generally a requirement, or necessity, and is missing. If I needed a screwdriver to assemble something but didn't have one, the project would grind to a halt until the need was met.

Desired or Required? There are two terms in the New Testament that are both often translated as "need," but there is an important distinction between them that Paul relies upon in this passage. It is akin to the difference in English between lack/shortage versus need. The former is quantifiable and does not refer to the total absence of something. The latter is generally not quantifiable; it's either there or it's not. Why is this distinction important here? When Paul talks about learning to be content in 4:10, he is talking about a lack or shortage. When he talks about God meeting needs, he is referring to that non-quantifiable must-have—the thing needed to accomplish a given task. The lack/shortage term can be thought of as something that is desired, not required. The other term most often refers to things that are necessary or required.

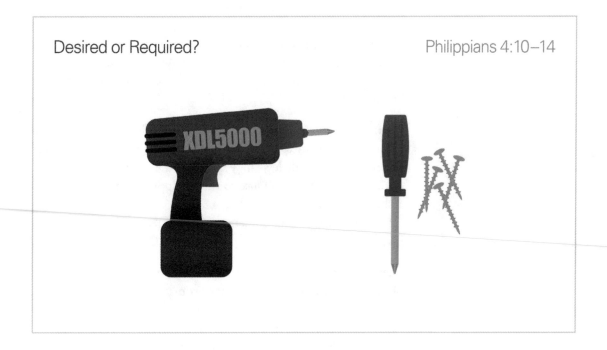

Desired or Required?   Philippians 4:10–14

As Paul talks about learning to be content in all sorts of circumstances, he uses the lack/shortage term to describe the situation (first in 4:11 and again in 4:12) to contrast having abundance and having a lack. Mark uses the same pairing of terms in 12:44 to describe the poor widow's offering of two small copper coins in comparison to that given by the rich. They gave out of their abundance, whereas she gave out of her lack. The term does not mean that she was utterly bereft; she had the two coins, after all. It simply characterizes her as having a shortage or lack. In other words, she didn't really have money to spare, whereas the rich had so much that their gift wouldn't have put a dent in their abundance.

In 4:10–14, Paul is concerned with the relationship between what we have/experience and how content we are—with emphasis on the latter in 4:11. He is not talking here about some *required* element, but a *desired* one. Having experienced both little and much, both hunger and being filled, both lack and abundance, Paul has learned an important lesson. Being content is not contingent upon having all that you want, but on being thankful and satisfied with what you have. The problem is that the more we get, the more we tend to want. If our contentedness is contingent upon our desires being met, then we are destined to be dissatisfied.

Paul makes clear in 4:18 that he is not writing from a deficit position, at least not anymore. The Philippians' gift has ensured he has abundance. In either case, he's learned not to base his satisfaction on his circumstances.

In 4:11, Paul used a connecting word that signaled a departure from his main argument to a sidebar that strengthens or supports what precedes it. "Nevertheless" in 4:14 signals the return to the big idea of the section: Paul's response to the Philippians' gift. It also marks a shift in terminology regarding *need*: He is no longer discussing a lack or shortage, but something that is required to accomplish his mission.

There are several extra references to the Philippians in the Greek of 4:15, variously translated as "you yourselves" and "Philippians." Neither is necessary in the context. The extra references are used here to slow the flow and build up to a significant statement. It's like us saying, "Alright folks," to gather attention. What's so important?

The critical role that the Philippians' gift has played in his ministry. It wasn't a matter of abundance versus lack but of moving forward versus grinding to a screeching halt.

Paul takes them back to the very beginning of his ministry after departing from Macedonia, using that as the framework for describing the significance of their gift. He then makes a statement that is false—at least, until you read both parts. He states that "no church" shared with him in the matter of giving and receiving, despite the fact that the Philippians indeed shared. Why bend the truth like this? To draw extra attention to the one exception to his negative statement. There was a church: It was the Philippians.

Who shared? In order to draw extra attention to the fact that the Philippians were the only church who shared in his ministry, Paul uses an old trick. He begins by making a false statement that no one shared with him, even though this is not the whole truth. By delaying the *rest of the story*, he skillfully casts them as the one notable exception.

Who shared?   Philippians 4:15

You alone!

No ~~church~~ shared with me

Paul could have simply stated that they were the only ones who helped, but this would have had much less of a rhetorical impact. This convention—where the negated statement is not actually true until you read the exception at the end—is used frequently in the New Testament (see Mark 6:5, where it says Jesus was unable to heal people in Nazareth). Framing the statement in this way draws extra attention to the excepted element. In this context, it drives home the point that the Philippians' gift made all the difference to his ministry.

In 4:16, Paul recalls that this sharing happened on more than one occasion! There is also a shift to the other term for "need," the required kind. This is *the need* their gift met, not an increased comfort or abundance for abundance's sake. Verse 17 shows that Paul is not seeking another gift by praising them, but wanting them to understand the difference it made for the kingdom—something for which the Lord will reward them.

After dismissing any confusion about whether he was thanking them and holding out his hand for more, Paul returns to his main line of thought in 4:18. He makes clear in this resumption that he not only has received their gift in its entirety, but that it has resulted in abundance for him. Epaphroditus has proven faithful with what he was entrusted to carry to Paul. And even though Paul knows how to be content without, having abundance is a welcome change from what he usually experienced (see 2 Cor 11:9).

The final sentence of 4:18 describes the resulting effect of receiving the gift carried by Epaphroditus: He's been made "full" or "complete." The term used here is different from the one used in 4:12 for the contrast with "hungry." It refers not just to being filled, but to being complete. The idea is that their gift has not just met his needs but has given him all things necessary to move forward with his ministry. The reference to "what you sent" sets the stage for Paul to recharacterize their gift using a loaded expression: "a fragrant offering, an acceptable sacrifice well-pleasing to God." Imagine the blessing it would have been to hear such a description, especially since their gift was sacrificially given out of their own lack (see 2 Cor 8:1–5).

Because Paul began by essentially downplaying the significance of their gift, he is able to heap rich praise upon them without them thinking he was asking for more. Although he alludes to receiving a reward in the long-term in 4:17, he does not neglect what can be expected currently. Paul makes reference at the end of 4:18 to being made full or complete. The same term is used in 4:19 to describe the promise that God will fill or fulfill their every need according to His riches in Christ Jesus. "Need" here refers to the required or essential elements, not to a shortage or lack. The fulfillment may result in an overwhelming abundance since it is based on God's riches in Christ, but the focus here is not on riches, comfort, or making someone wealthy. Instead, the idea is that as we sacrificially give to meet the required needs of ministry, God Himself will see that our own required needs are met. There is no hint that a prosperity gospel is being taught here. This derives from a fundamental misunderstanding of Paul's distinction between what is desired and what is required. What is required is in focus here.

Paul closes this section with a doxology that focuses on God as our Father—the provider of all things that we need. The giving and faithful stewardship of gifts is not about earning His favor or approval. Instead, sacrificial obedience—by both the giver and the receiver— results in God receiving the glory that He so richly deserves. He is not just worthy of our worship, but also of our humble obedience.

Philippians 4:21–23

Paul ends the letter like he began it. Just as he addresses all the saints in Christ Jesus in the opening, he sends greetings to them all in the closing. As he let them know at the outset that he was not alone in sending the letter, he includes greetings from those with him. Paul once again singles out a politically well-connected group like he did in 1:13. Paul does more than just refer to those who have heard the gospel, like he did in 1:13; here he refers to those who have responded positively to it. There is debate as to exactly who this refers to, but there is little doubt as to why he includes it. Recall that the letter opened by addressing doubts the Philippians had about the advancement of the gospel with Paul in prison. Mentioning this particular group of believers would have offered further evidence to allay their fears about Paul's gospel ministry. Finally, he ends where he began with his reference to the grace of the Lord Jesus Christ. Although this is a standard way of signing off, it rounds out the close connections to his greeting.

Final Reflections

Paul's letter to the Philippians is more than a theological treatise. It's also about more than suffering, thankfulness, and the incarnation. His discussion of suffering stemmed from his present circumstances; his choice to rejoice was an improbable response. Paul followed the example of Jesus by humbling himself—he was willing to be humiliated. We're called to do the same.

Philippians shows us Paul's deep concern for the church. This concern is exemplified throughout the letter by his challenge to esteem others. The climax of this is the public call for Euodia and Syntyche to move beyond the status quo of some unresolved conflict. Again, we're called to do the same.

The exhortations of Philippians are carefully framed as timeless principles rather than time-bound rules. Let's live what Paul professed.

Subject and Author Index

A

achievement 86–87
anxiety 102–03
assurance (of salvation), *see* eternal
    security
attitude 55–56, 71–72
    in the face of dire circum-
        stances 13–14

B

Barnabas 57
boasting 75–77
    and personal identity 78
burnout (in ministry) 29, 42, 86

C

Clement 107
conflict (interpersonal) 97–99
contentment 114

D

dark night of the soul 22
death:
    deeds worthy of 93, 94
    exaltation through 24, 25–29
    of Jesus 48, 81, 82

E

Elliot, Jim 79
Epaphroditus 8, 51, 57, 63, 66, 71,
    100, 107, 110, 111
    sickness of 63–65
Euodia 8, 91, 97, 98, 100, 107, 119;
    see also Syntyche
eternal security 52
exaltation (after humiliation)
    48–49, 50

F

fellowship (between Christians)
    41, 49; *see also* conflict

G

gentleness 101
God:
    absence/distance of 14, 17–18
    attributes of 10
    as basis of joy 22
    calling of 33
    faithfulness of 22
    "good work" of 10–11, 22
    perspective of 14, 34, 35
    right view of 53–54

trust in 22–23
ways of referring to 10–11
gospel:
    advancement of 9, 10, 14, 18, 19, 22, 24, 28, 56, 61, 78, 100, 117
    enemies of 91–92, 94
    life worthy of 31, 51, 52, 99, 100
    motivations for preaching 17, 19–21
    opposition to 32, 33, 94
    prosperity gospel 115
    sharing in 109
grace 9, 35, 65, 117
greeting (of a letter) 9

H

heaven 27
Hendricks, Howard 106
Holy Spirit 23, 73
    fellowship of 39
humility 52

I

identity 78–79
introduction
    of Pauline letters 7–8
    of Philippians 7–11, 13

J

Jesus:
    call of 17
    death of 46, 47
    divinity of 45–47
    exaltation of 48–49, 50, 51
    humanity of 46–47
    humility of 45–50, 51
        as example 49–50, 97
    incarnation of 48, 119
    obedience of 82, 97
    resurrection of 81, 82
    return of 102
    service to 92
    suffering of 81–82
    transformation into the image of 93

John Mark (nephew of Barnabas) 57

K

kingdom of God 81, 92, 114

L

leadership 67
legalism 105–06
love:
    of Christians 11
    consolation of 39
    as motivation 82
    preaching the gospel from 17
    unity of 41, 43

O

obedience 50, 51, 115
    of Jesus 82, 97
    motivations for 56
    to Pharisaic code 76

P

Paul:
    boasting of 75–78
    and conflict resolution 97, 99
    credentials of 7–9
    defense of the gospel 17, 22, 24
    deliverance of 23–24
    imitation of 91, 107
    imprisonment of 13–14, 15, 17–18, 19, 21–22, 24, 27, 28, 32, 34, 60
    persecution of 27
    prayers of 9–10
    past regrets of 85–86
    as slave of Christ 8–9
    support of 109–10
    tone of letters of 89–90
    view of life and death of 26–28
peace of God 102–03
prayer:
    as basis for confidence 23
    for deliverance 14
    intercessory prayer 23
    of Paul 10–11
    and thanksgiving 103

principles for living 106–08

R

regret 85

rejoicing 98, 101
    despite circumstances 9,
      20–22, 97, 119
    and complaining 55–56, 72–73
    importance of 71
    and resentment 101–02
    as safeguard 52, 72–73,
      101–02, 103
    and suffering 56

righteousness 83
    of God 92
    from faith 81–82, 83
    fruit of 11
    self-righteousness 56, 81
    works-based righteousness
      76, 83

S

salvation 33, 82
    "working out with fear and
      trembling" 52, 54

self-esteem 53

shame (in Graeco-Roman culture)
   64, 101, 102

sin 81
    confession of 23
    freedom from the power of 81
    sin nature 48, 81

Syntyche 8, 91, 97, 98, 100, 107,
   119; *see also* Euodia

suffering 34–35, 54, 55, 119
    of Jesus 81–82
    and the purposes of God 56

T

thankfulness 22, 55, 72, 103, 119
    and hospitality 109–10

Timothy 57–61, 66, 71, 100, 107

Titus 107

transformation 93

trust 22, 102

U

unity 32, 43, 98
    basis of 41

Scripture Index

Old Testament

Leviticus
12:3 76

Psalms
73:21–22............... 14

Proverbs
3:5–6..................... 22
13:12.....................99
17:2........................8
19:10 8

New Testament

Matthew
6:33......................92
15:18.....................72

Mark
6:5 113
12:44...................112

Luke
6:43–45.................72
11:42 107
12:44....................112
18:18–25 99

John..................90
15:1–6 52
15:5 53

Acts...................107
15:36–51 57

Romans
1:32 93
3:23.....................83
4:4–5.....................82
12:10 61
16:17 94

1 Corinthians 91
1:12 97
5:1.......................97
11:1......................107

2 Corinthians 92
2:1–8 97
11:4......................94
11:9......................114
11:23–29 27

Galatians 7, 91
1:6 94
1:6–10 97
1:11–2:14..............107

Ephesians
2:10 52
4:29 106

Philippians.........107
1 56
1:1 8
1:1–11 7–11
1:2 9
1:3 9
1:5 ....10, 109
1:6 ....9, 10, 11, 13,
                    22, 23
1:7 ....9, 11
1:9 ....9, 11
1:9–11....................11
1:10 ....11, 97
1:12 ....14, 15, 22,
                    34, 101
1:12–18 34
1:12–21 20
1:13 ....15, 117
1:14 ....16, 17
1:15 ....16, 22
1:15–17 16–18
1:16 24
1:17 16
1:18 ......19–20, 21, 24,
                    28, 71, 97
1:18–20 19–24

1:18–26 18
1:19 .... 23, 24
1:19–20 34
1:20 .... 23, 25
1:21 .... 56, 79
1:21–24 26–29
1:21–26 24
1:22 .... 26, 27, 28
1:23 27
1:24 .... 26, 28
1:25–26 97
1:27 ...... 32, 33, 51, 100
1:27–28 34
1:27–30 .... 31–35, 97
1:28 .... 33, 34
1:29 34
1:29–30 .... 34, 54
1:30 34
2:1 .... 39–40, 51
2:1–2 40
2:1–4 .... 39–43, 97
2:2 ...... 40, 52, 97, 100
2:2–4 41
2:3 .... 42, 52
2:3–4 .... 41, 42, 97
2:4 .... 28, 42, 43
2:5–11 .. 29, 45–50, 82,
             97
2:6–7 46
2:6–11 48
2:7 47
2:7–8 47
2:8 47
2:9 35
2:10 49
2:10–11 93
2:12 .... 51, 52, 86
2:12–13 54
2:12–18 51–56
2:14 .... 54, 55
2:15–16 56
2:16 56
2:17 56
2:17–18 71
2:18 56
2:19–22 .... 58, 66

2:19–24 ...... 57–61, 64
2:20 59
2:21 59
2:22 59
2:23 59
2:23–24 60
2:25 .... 59, 66
2:25–30 ...... 63–67, 111
3:1 .... 97, 101, 102, 105
3:1–2 72
3:1–4 71–74
3:2 .... 73, 77
3:2–3 75
3:3 .... 73, 77
3:4 75
3:4–6 76
3:4–11 75–82
3:6 81
3:7 78
3:8 79
3:8–11 83
3:9 .... 80, 83
3:9–10 81
3:10–11 82
3:11 .... 82, 83
3:12 ...... 83, 84, 86, 89
3:12–14 79
3:13 .... 84, 85
3:13–14 ..... 84, 85, 102
3:14 .... 84, 86
3:15 .... 89–90, 91
3:15–21 89–94
3:16 91
3:17 .... 8, 91
3:18 .... 91, 92
3:19–20 93
3:19–21 92
3:20 92
3:20–21 83
4 .... 91, 99, 100
4:1 100
4:1–3 98
4:1–7 97–103
4:2 .... 91, 97
4:2–3 101
4:3 100

4:4 101–02
4:5 101
4:6 102
4:6–7 103
4:7 103
4:8 106
4:8–9 105–08
4:9 107
4:10 110
4:10–14 .... 111, 112
4:10–20 109–15
4:11 .... 111, 112
4:12 112
4:13 53
4:15 .... 112, 113
4:16 .... 111, 114
4:17 114
4:18 .... 112, 114
4:21–23 117
4:29–30 13

1 Thessalonians
5:11 .... 58, 61

1 Timothy
1:3 94
1:3–4 97
3:6 58
6:3 94

Philemon 8, 97

Hebrews 90
9:28 83

James
1:13–14 85
4:1–2 99
4:10 50

1 Peter
2:9 53
5:6 50

Revelation
7:16–17 27

About the Author

Steven E. Runge serves as a scholar-in-residence at Logos Bible Software. He has a Doctor of Literature degree in Biblical Languages from the University of Stellenbosch in South Africa, supervised by Christo Van der Merwe. He currently serves as a research associate affiliated with the Department of Ancient Studies, University of Stellenbosch. In preparation for his doctoral research, Steve completed several years of study in the linguistic fields of pragmatics and discourse grammar. This culminated in attending a workshop on discourse analysis offered by SIL/Wycliffe Bible Translators, facilitated by Stephen H. Levinsohn. He has also earned a Master of Theological Studies degree in Biblical Languages from Trinity Western Seminary in Langley, B.C., and a BA in Speech Communication from Western Washington University.

Steve has served as a visiting professor teaching Greek discourse grammar at Knox Theological Seminary; Dallas Theological Seminary, Wycliffe Hall, Oxford; Wales Evangelical School of Theology; and Southern Baptist Theological Seminary, besides offering exegesis workshops for pastors. While completing his education Steve served as an adjunct faculty member at Northwest Baptist Theological College, Trinity Western University, and Associated Canadian Theological Schools (ACTS). He and his wife were married in 1990. They have two daughters and live in Bellingham.

Like the graphics?
Share them.

The electronic edition of *High Definition Commentary: Philippians*, available for Logos Bible Software, includes ready-to-use versions of all the graphics for use in Proclaim, PowerPoint, and Keynote.

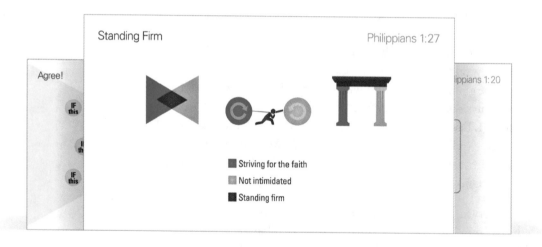

Understand the original meaning of the New Testament

Analyze it with the Greek New Testament Discourse Bundle.

Master original-language study with these resources, designed for the Logos Bible Software platform. Whether you're a seasoned Greek scholar or a first-time student, you'll gain insight into the authors' original intent with Dr. Steve Runge's pioneering scholarship.

What you'll get:

Tagged Greek & English texts, side by side for insightful study	Expositional commentaries based on discourse analysis
Text divided into preachable chunks	Custom-designed graphics for Bible teachers

Start understanding the New Testament like its original readers

Logos.com/DGNT • 1-800-875-6467 (US) • +1 360-527-1700 (Int'l)